GOOD·OLD·DAYS

I'll Be Home
for
Christmas™

Edited by Ken and Janice Tate

HOUSE of
WHITE
BIRCHES
PUBLISHERS
SINCE 1947

I'll Be Home for Christmas™

Editors: Ken and Janice Tate
Managing Editor: Barb Sprunger
Associate Editor: Kelly Keim
Editorial Assistant: Joanne Neuenschwander
Copy Editors: Nicki Lehman,
Mary Martin, Läna Schurb
Assistant Editors: Marla Freeman, Marj Morgan
Publication Coordinator: Tanya Turner

Graphic Arts Supervisor: Ronda Bechinski
Design/Production Artist: Erin Augsburger
Cover Design: Jessi Butler
Traffic Coordinator: Sandra Beres
Production Assistants: Janet Bowers, Chad Tate
Photography: Jeff Chilcote, Tammy Christian,
Kelly Heydinger
Photography Assistant: Linda Quinlan

Publishers: Carl H. Muselman, Arthur K. Muselman
Chief Executive Officer: John Robinson
Publishing Marketing Director: David McKee
Book Marketing Manager: Craig Scott
Product Development Director: Vivian Rothe
Publishing Services Director: Brenda Wendling
Publishing Services Manager: Brenda Gallmeyer

Printed in the United States of America
First Printing: 2002
Library of Congress Number: 2002103155
ISBN: 1-882138-90-2
Customer Service: (800) 829-5865

Every effort has been made to ensure the accuracy of the material in this book.
However, the publisher is not responsible for research errors or typographical mistakes in this publication.

We would like to thank the following for the art prints used in this book.

For fine-art prints and more information on the artists featured in *I'll Be Home for Christmas*, contact:

Tom Browning, Sisters, OR 97759, (541) 549-4365
Curtis Publishing, Indianapolis, IN 46202, (317) 633-2070, www.curtispublishing.com
Mill Pond Press Inc., Venice, FL 34292, (800) 535-0331
Norman Rockwell Family Trust, LaGrangeville, NY 12540 (845) 454-0859
John Sloane, Kirkland, IL 60146 (815) 522-6162
Wild Wings Inc., Lake City, MN 55041, (800) 445-4833

Dear Friends of the Good Old Days,

   Christmas in the Good Old Days was a time of giving, a time of sharing—a time of reflecting on what was really important. It was a time when our hearts were drawn back to home and hearth like no other.

   Every time I think of being home for Christmas, I remember the days when gifts were valued like gold, even though they were bought in pennies. Every tree was as spectacular as the national Christmas tree, even though it might be garlanded in popcorn rather than tinsel. Every Christmas season in my mind's eye was white, even though I know some were just cold.

   When it comes to Christmas and home, our memories have sentimental ways of playing tricks on us. Take for example my red Santa Christmas ornament.

   I don't know exactly how it became "my" ornament. Mama and Daddy had had it since the days of my older brother's infancy, but somehow it became mine.

   To me, that little Santa was the most beautiful ornament on the tree. He was bright red, with a full white beard and carried a huge sack slung over his back. After we got electricity, I realized that the sack was actually a receptacle for a bulb from our single strand of lights. With the bulb inserted, my little Santa glowed brighter than anything else on our tree.

   Trimming the tree, that great Christmas tradition, became even greater in my eyes. Brother Dennis always got to top the tree with the star, but to me I got the coup de grace. After the tree was trimmed to perfection and had passed inspection by Mama and Daddy, I ceremoniously pulled my Santa from where I had hidden him for just this event. Stepping forward with much show and fanfare, I hung him near a bulb, slipped the bulb into his sack and stepped back. Now the tree could be lit.

   The little boy who so loved to watch his Santa glow grew up, got married and started a family of his own. Over the process of decades "he" became me. My wife Janice and I moved half a continent away only to find ourselves drawn back home from time to time.

   On one visit not long after our silver anniversary, I was moved to ask Mama about my beautiful little red Santa. She went to a closet and pulled down the box of Christmas fixtures. There, wrapped delicately in tissue was my Santa. He was smaller than I remembered, and his paint was faded markedly. I just knew he was made of fine porcelain, but he actually was made of plastic. The sack receptacle was curled a bit from a too-hot bulb.

   Mama hadn't had a tree since Daddy's death, and the box of ornaments had sat unused. "Do you want to keep him?" she asked. I thought about it, but then decided against it. In my mind's eye he would always be perfect—bright and shiny and glowing warmly. I don't know where he is today, but in memory he'll always be in the hands of a little boy proudly hanging him on a perfect tree surrounded by perfect gifts with a perfect white snow adorning the landscape outside the windows.

   And that's the way Christmas memories of home and hearth should be—perfect. As we begin this trek back to the perfect holidays of our youth, leave behind the commercial baggage of Christmas today. Board the train, load up the Lizzie and jump in the sleigh. Our destination is just over the ridge and we'll be there by dark. The trek may be many miles and many years in the making, but join me.
I'll be home for Christmas.

Ken Tate

Contents

Going Home • 6

Gifts of the Heart • 38

Home for the Holidays • 64

© John Sloane

Going Home

Chapter One

What is it about Christmas that makes a person yearn for the old home place? In the "Good Old Days," going home might mean a short sleigh ride down a snowy country lane—or an even shorter ride in one of those "new-fangled" carriages called automobiles. Even in today's frenetic world, the emotion of returning to hearth and home, kith and kin, is still a powerful magnet.

When Janice and I were youngsters, however, the draw of going home in the yule season seemed all the more powerful. Why? I guess there might be several reasons.

For one thing, we weren't so far flung as we are today. Out of the 11 children my Grandma and Grandpa Tate raised to adulthood, eight lived in the same county all their lives and two others lived in adjoining counties. Only one, my Uncle Harley, moved out of the Ozark Mountains in southern Missouri we all called home; he moved to Belton, Mo., to be near the "big city"—Kansas City.

Janice's father lived on the hilltop above the valley in which he had been born. From their home on the highest ridge for miles Janice's mother could see the edge of the town she was raised in, only about 12 miles away as the crow flies.

Janice and I lived for years away from home before the magnet pulled us back. We returned to raise our children on Janice's old home place; the home she was born in will be the last home, God willing, either of us ever knows. The small frame house we both love so well is just a few miles from the farm where I was raised.

Not all families had the blessing of living so close together as ours, however. For them, I'm sure the pull of going home was even greater. Hundreds of thousands were driven from the farm by Depression and war during the first half of the 20th century. For them, the deep yearning to see Mama and Daddy was all the stronger as the holidays approached.

So, as December waned, families from far and wide boxed up a whole year's worth of love, along with a carload of presents and food, and headed back to their roots.

Telephone service still wasn't a common thing out on the farm, and photographs were not snapped nearly as often. So often letters were the only connection with relatives left so untouchable by miles and circumstances.

So, as sons and daughters headed home for holidays, they brought with them children who had never been held by grandparents. Growth was measured year by year as those children grew up. And every season brought more gray hair to those dear heads of the family.

There never seemed to be enough time to catch up in those fleeting days. After all, there were so many tales to tell, memories to make, traditions to entrust to another generation. Before any of us knew what had happened, the time was gone.

These are the stories of those Christmas treks back to the old home place, whether near or far. It's just a few more miles; jump in the sleigh and join us. We're going home.

—*Ken Tate*

Billy's Christmas Gifts

By Laura Clark

I was 14 on that Christmas long ago. We were anxiously awaiting word from my oldest brother, Billy, who had gone off and joined the Army several months before. He was due home Christmas Eve on his first leave. Daddy had met the bus he should have been on, but there was no Billy, and there would not be another bus until the next day.

Mama was sure something terrible had happened. Daddy said she shouldn't carry on so; the boy was old enough to take care of himself. But he didn't sound any too certain.

As for me, I divided my time between worrying about Billy and worrying about myself. I was at an age where I was very unhappy with my looks. We had a wardrobe with two mirrors and I spent a lot of time standing in front of it, staring first into one mirror and then the other. I was terribly worried. Neither mirror convinced me that I was becoming the beautiful girl I wanted to be. In fact, just the opposite was true; I was getting plainer each day.

While I was contemplating my fate, I heard a car horn. It was my Uncle Tasker, driving the black panel truck he used to deliver dry cleaning. By now it was late Christmas Eve, and we wondered why he was visiting so late. I opened my bedroom window and looked out. Mama and Daddy had gone out to the truck.

"I brought you a Christmas present," Tasker said to them.

"What is it?" Mama asked excitedly.

"It's in the back of the truck," he told them.

Mama hurried around to the back, but before she got there, the doors flew open and Billy jumped out.

Everyone hugged him and asked questions. Why was he so late? Why hadn't he been on the bus? Why was he with Tasker?

The answer was simple. He had spent all his money on Christmas gifts, and he had had to hitchhike. He had made it to Tasker's house and had asked him to bring him the rest of the way to our farm.

What a Christmas Eve we had! Billy carried a large duffel bag and a small suitcase. He began pulling Christmas gifts out of the duffel bag. There were presents for everyone. In those days, in rural North Carolina, we had very few Christmas gifts, so we were very excited when Billy distributed all those gaily wrapped packages.

"Where are your clothes? Let me hang them up for you," Mama said.

"I didn't have room for any clothes. The gifts took up all the room," Billy laughed.

"What on earth are you going to wear?" Mama asked, looking worried.

"He might be able to wear some of my clothes," Tasker offered.

"Mine would come nearer fitting him," my brother Joe spoke up.

"I'm sure we'll find something. At least you're home. That's the main thing," Mama said.

By that time I had opened my gift. It was a shiny new watch. I couldn't believe it was for me. I would be the only girl in my class with a watch. How proud I was!

All the others got nice gifts, too. I think there was a doll for Mary. The twins, Milton and Melvin, got air rifles. Mama got a radio. I can't remember what Daddy or Joe got. I believe Harold got a dump truck. Then there were presents for other relatives. Billy had been saving for months to buy all those gifts.

But Billy still didn't have any clothes to wear. Everyone was willing to lend him anything they could, but back then, people didn't have lots of extra clothes, so there weren't many to be lent.

Billy was taller than Joe, so Joe's clothes didn't fit him any too good. But I don't think he minded at all. When his old school friends and neighbors came to welcome him home, they didn't seem to notice that his pants were too short or that his shirtsleeves didn't come down as far as they should. When we went

1941 *Household Magazine*, House of White Birches nostalgia archives

someplace where he didn't want to be seen in his ill-fitting clothes, Mama washed the clothes he had worn home. But for the most part, Billy didn't mind that his clothes didn't fit very well. To him, it was more important to bring gifts for all of us.

As for me, that watch was just what I needed to boost my morale. After that, when I stood in front of the mirror, I didn't seem so plain any more. It was surprising how the shiny watch on my wrist improved my looks—at least, in my own estimation. ❄

The Spirit of Christmas

By Clara M. Parker

I will never forget the lesson of love we learned one yule season long ago. It was Christmas Eve. Aunt Lizzy, Uncle Ben, our cousins, our mother Annie and we four kids were busy getting ready to trim the tree. A cheery fire in the fireplace sent up little spurts of colored flame as the logs settled.

Outside it was snowing. Great, fluffy flakes drifted down to settle on the sidewalks. Drifts were beginning to pile up. I pushed the lace curtains aside and watched the winter wonderland through the frosted panes, my head scarcely higher than the windowsill.

My father's footprints on the sidewalk and front steps were rapidly disappearing in the new-fallen snow. Just moments before, he had come huffing and puffing up the steps, stomped the snow from his overshoes, shook it from his derby hat and the velvet collar of his Chesterfield overcoat, and entered the warm living room.

He had taken a later train than we had and had been delayed by the snow all along the route. Unable to hire a hack, he had struggled through the snow on foot all the way from the train station. Now he was sitting near the fireplace, stretching his cold feet toward the flames and rubbing his fingers to start the circulation.

For Mother and us children, it had been an all-day trip from Champaign to Collinsville by the early train. The distance was not great, but there was a four-hour layover between trains at Clinton. A potbellied stove belched forth enough heat from its bulging, cherry-red middle to warm the train station's waiting room. The whole room steamed. Puddles of melting snow covered the wooden floor. The wooden-slat benches were hard, and the wrought-iron arms were so close together that there was scarcely room for the well-bundled children to sit, let alone an adult. The odor of wet wool and rubber overshoes filled the room.

Four hours of waiting! Luggage! Snow-covered platform! Icy train steps! Steamy, over-heated passenger coaches! More hard seats, covered with scratchy green plush! Tickets! Mittens, mufflers, leggings, overshoes and overcoats to be removed from squirming, impatient bodies! Four restless, excited children! Tomorrow was Christmas!

Herding us four youngsters on a train trip under such circumstances was not easy. Keeping us quietly occupied during the long layover in the little station was tiring, but my mother did her best with stories and guessing games she invented on the spur of the moment. She endured it all in order spend Christmas with her sister Liz and her family.

Now at our destination and with Father safe and sound, the warm room, sweetly scented with the outdoorsy pine fragrance from the Christmas tree, made Mother drowsy, but our shouts and laughter kept her awake.

When Aunt Liz pushed open the sliding doors between the living and dining rooms and announced dinner, we all trooped into the dining room and found our places at the table. Uncle Ben, in his best stentorian manner, said grace. Aunt Liz served.

A large beef potpie was the main dish. Its mouth-watering fragrance filled the room as the crust was punctured. Aunt Liz ladled a generous portion of steaming brown beef, little golden carrots, baby onions and flaky crust smothered in rich, brown gravy onto each plate. We were offered our choice of milk or home-canned tomato juice. Several kinds of pickles, watermelon-rind pickles, corn relish and currant jelly were passed. There were spiced peaches and preserves, all home-canned. Dessert was a red devil's food cake slathered with white boiled frosting.

Trimming the tree would be difficult after

this repast, but we children were so excited at the prospect of Santa Claus coming that we gave the adults no rest. At last all the ornaments were hung, and the last of the popcorn and cranberry garlands was draped in place. All the little twisted wax candles were fastened by their small metal clips. It was time to light the tree.

Uncle Ben carefully applied a lighted match to the wick of each candle and stepped back to admire the effect. It was beautiful! It was magical! For a breathless moment, we children were quiet, awed by the beauty of the decorated, lighted Christmas tree. The glow from the dying fire and the flickering light of many candles cast long shadows of the people who were sitting on the floor, admiring the tree.

Aunt Lizzy went to the piano and played *Silent Night* as we all sang along. Uncle Ben then picked up a worn volume of Dickens and read a passage about Tiny Tim from *A Christmas Carol*. An ardent student of Shakespeare, he had longed for the stage; now, he satisfied such yearnings by pleading cases in court. He had a beautiful voice, and we were all spellbound as we listened to him read.

Suddenly the doorbell rang.

A stranger in a threadbare overcoat stood at the door. The snow blew in around him.

"Please forgive me for intruding," the stranger said. "I no longer have a home. As I struggled through the snow I heard the carol and was touched by the peacefulness of your home. I remembered other Christmases long gone. May I join you?"

The door opened wide. With a theatrical wave of his arm, Uncle Ben ushered the stranger inside, close to the dying embers, and threw another log on the fire. My mother and Aunt Liz rushed to the kitchen to prepare that panacea for all human ills—warm food. We children crowded around the visitor, telling him about our train trip, of the tree trimming, of the snow, and that Santa was coming.

After the stranger had eaten his fill and we had all returned to the living room, we again began to sing Christmas carols. Suddenly the room swelled with the music as the stranger joined in. In perfect harmony, he and Uncle Ben sang and sang. Once upon a time, people must have paid dearly for the privilege of hearing that remarkable voice.

Suddenly, as quickly as he had come, the stranger departed.

"Thank you!" he said. "Thank you one and all. You have no idea what you have done for me this night. Merry Christmas and may God bless you all."

The swirling snow swallowed him up in the night. That was long ago, but I have never forgotten that lesson of love taught by the spirit of Christmas in the Good Old Days. ✳

Going Home For Christmas

By Edgar A. Guest

He little knew the sorrow that was in his vacant chair;
He never guessed they'd miss him, or he'd surely have been there;
He couldn't see his mother or the lump that filled her throat,
Or the tears that started falling as she read his hasty note;
And he couldn't see his father, sitting sorrowful and dumb,
Or he never would have written that he thought he couldn't come.

He little knew the gladness that his presence would have made,
And the joy it would have given, or he never would have stayed.
He didn't know how hungry had the little mother grown
Once again to see her baby and to claim him for her own.
He didn't guess the meaning of his visit Christmas Day
Or he never would have written that he couldn't get away.

He couldn't see the fading of the cheeks that once were pink,
And the silver in the tresses; and he didn't stop to think
How the years are passing swiftly, and next Christmas it might be
There would be no home to visit and no mother dear to see.
He didn't think about it—I'll not say he didn't care.
He was heedless and forgetful or he'd surely have been there.

Are you going home for Christmas? Have you written you'll be there?
Going home to kiss the mother and to show her that you care?
Going home to greet the father in a way to make him glad?
If you're not I hope there'll never come a time you'll wish you had.
Just sit down and write a letter—it will make their heart strings hum
With a tune of perfect gladness—if you'll tell them that you'll come.

1927 *Farmer's Wife Magazine*,
House of White Birches nostalgia archives

Christmas in Georgia

By Mary Moore Campbell

By now all the Christmases of my childhood are rolled into one, but I particularly remember the Christmas of 1920. I was 10 years old. That year stands out because Dee, my youngest uncle, had come home. For the past two years he had been in France, fighting in World War I to "make the world safe for democracy." Now he was back and everybody in the family was determined to make this the very best Christmas ever.

Our extended family included my mother and father and their three children, of whom I was youngest. Then there was Uncle, my mother's older brother and titular head of the family, his wife Rene and their two children, Virginia and Buddy. Auntie, my mother's youngest sister, was unmarried and still lived at home. Dee was the baby of the family and, as I said, had just returned from the war.

Each year we went home for Christmas at my mother's old home place. It was a big rambling house built before the Civil War in the Garden Valley section of Macon County, Ga. My mother, older brothers Cleve and Sidney, and I always joined the others there several days before Christmas. My father was a lawyer in Montezuma, a town 15 miles away, and he came out on Christmas Eve. Life was less complicated then and this was the happiest time of the year.

First on the agenda was selecting and cutting the tree. This meant several scouting trips to the woods for the boys to find the perfect tree. It had to be a holly tree with plenty of berries, it had to be symmetrical and tall enough to reach the ceiling. When they found the tree that Uncle had long ago selected, we all loaded into a two-horse wagon with an ax and a saw, and went to get it.

In central Georgia we seldom have snow. But it was cold, and we laughed and sang as the dry leaves blew, squirrels skittered, birds called, and dogs ran and barked. When we got back from the woods, the tree was set up in the off-parlor by means of crossbars nailed to the bottom. It was also supported by a piece of picture wire wrapped around the trunk of the tree about two-thirds up and attached to the wall.

After supper, with a roaring oak-log fire going in the fireplace, we set about decorating the tree. Aunt Rene brought down from upstairs the box of tinsel and baubles that were used year after year. As always, various of the adults had a few new baubles that had struck their fancy to add to the store, and Uncle had remembered to get the tiny candles for the candle holders that clamped onto the branches. These had to be put on last and had to be placed very carefully so that they were accessible and safe. They would be lit on Christmas morning. When it was finished, the tree was a work of art.

In all my life I have not seen anything prettier than that tree. To my 10-year-old eyes, its height was more impressive than the California redwoods. The leaves were such a rich, dark, glossy green and the berries were so red! The alternating rows of gold and silver tinsel, the tiny hanging wreaths, the angels, balls, stars and flower-filled baskets, all caught in the dancing light from the fireplace, were beautiful enough to thrill a little girl's heart for a lifetime.

The next day Cleve and Sidney, with all the help they could muster among the hired hands, started gathering material for the Christmas Eve bonfire. They wanted this to be the biggest, best bonfire we had ever had. They said they wanted to light up Macon County.

The following days were busy ones, but by dusk on Christmas Eve, everything was ready and the last-minute shoppers had returned from town. Fires roared in the fireplaces as supper cooked. Everything smelled like Christmas, and everyone was ready for the holiday. Even the little ones felt the excitement. Uncle and Dee checked on the hired hands to be sure all the chores were done and the stock fed. Daddy tried to get a setback game started and the boys were urging the cooks, one regular and one "company," to put supper on the table so we could get through with it and set the bonfire.

Finally we sat down to supper. By expanding the old oak table as far as it would go and by setting up a smaller table to one side, we were all able to eat at one time, and that was good, because often we children had to wait for the second table. The table was loaded with large platters of country-fried steak, fried ham and fried sweet potatoes. There were big bowls of grits and scrambled eggs, and as a special treat for Christmas, there was a large baking dish of scalloped oysters. There were smaller dishes of fig preserves and plum sauce, and molds of blackberry jelly and apple jelly. Algia and Dora, the cooks, kept the plates of big, fat biscuits and lacy-edged corn bread coming as long as anybody could poke in another mouthful.

As soon as we left the table, Cleve and Sidney started trying to marshal the crowd toward the bonfire, but the grown-ups would not be rushed. They were savoring every minute of the celebration. Aunt Rene put nightclothes on three-year-old Virginia and baby Buddy and wrapped them in blankets. She carried Virginia and Auntie carried Buddy. Uncle and Daddy had their arms full of fireworks and my mother carried a chair. Dee had gone on ahead with the boys to set the fire.

The moon was shining, the dogs were barking, and the hands, with their wives and children, had already gathered off to one side, waiting for the fun to start. To me, the pile looked tremendous. It was in the middle of an open field several hundred yards from the house and the oak grove in front of the house. As the old, dry wood and the fat lightwood stumps caught fire, the flames seemed to leap all the way to the moon.

Then came the fireworks. All I was allowed to handle were Roman candles and sparklers. Cleve and Sidney had 1-inch, 2-inch and 5-inch penny crackers by the handful. There were also cherry bombs, thunderbolts, pinwheels, skyrockets, and three-stand and five-stand double shots. Whenever things quieted down a little, somebody would throw a full packet of Japanese penny crackers into the fire.

Neighbors came and passersby stopped. Some frightened children cried, the dogs howled, the teenagers shouted, the grown-ups laughed and talked, and still the firecrackers popped. After the women had gone in (taking me with them, to my disgust) and the men had cleared around the dying fire to be sure it was safe, the boys were *still* throwing penny crackers into the embers.

Soon after we went in, Virginia, Buddy and I hung up our stockings for Santa Claus and were put to bed. (Would you believe that at 10, I still believed in Santa Claus? Children were not as sophisticated then as they are now.) After Cleve and Sidney were sent to bed, the grown-ups had eggnog and fruitcake, played setback and talked about old times far into the night.

Christmas Day was truly a day to remember. We were up long before daylight to see if Santa Claus really had come. He had. That was the year he brought me a white dresser with pink flowers to match the doll bed and wardrobe that he had brought the year before. Of course, everybody had to get up to watch us take the gifts out of the stockings. Mixed in with the gifts were fruits and candies. I especially remember the raisins in bunches with seeds still in them.

They were wrapped in white tissue and tied with red ribbon.

After the stockings came breakfast, and then we all filed into the parlor to take the gifts off the tree. The tree was loaded down because everybody gave everybody a gift. There was no drawing of names like family groups do now. My mother always gave me $1 to buy gifts, and I made it go around. I still remember the thought, planning and anguish that went into the choice of gifts. Dee handed out the gifts, watching to see that nobody got left out. Finally, the last gift was off the tree and the wrapping papers were picked up and carried out.

All morning, everyone—even the servants and the field hands who had come up to the big house for their tot of Christmas cheer—was slipping around corners and jumping out from unexpected places, saying, "Good morning! Christmas gift!" The one who greeted first earned a gift from the one who was caught.

Then came Christmas dinner! Of course, there was turkey and dressing with giblet gravy, rice and cranberry sauce. But that was only the beginning. Other meats included sliced, baked pork; ham with barbecue sauce; sliced, boiled, country-cured ham; meat loaf made of home-ground round steak seasoned with enough hot red pepper to burn the eyeballs (because that was the way Uncle and Dee liked it); chicken pie with blackberry jelly for my daddy; chicken salad for Auntie; and sliced souse with vinegar. On one large tray were six or more kinds of pickles and relishes, including brandied peaches.

For salads we had a choice of congealed fruit salad (made with acidulated gelatin, because this was before the days of Jell-O), Waldorf salad made with black walnuts, and cabbage slaw. Casseroles of sweet potato soufflé full of raisins and nuts and topped with marsh-mallows, macaroni and cheese, and creamed asparagus were passed and passed again. One large platter had whipped potatoes piled around the outside and the middle filled with creamed peas. Fresh young turnip greens and green beans were also on the menu. Beaten biscuits were served to go with the salad, pone corn bread to go with the vegetables, and homemade yeast rolls to go with the meat.

The desserts were ambrosia made of oranges and fresh coconut, topped with whipped cream and a cherry, and every kind of cake imaginable. The fruitcakes, dark and light, had been made before Thanksgiving and stored in metal containers (50-pound lard cans, actually), surrounded by apples and liberally doused with wine periodically so that they would be moist. Everybody had a favorite cake and everybody's favorite had been made, including Japanese fruitcake for me and pound cake for Uncle.

Some of the others were fresh coconut with raisins and fresh coconut with nuts; chocolate cake with white layers and chocolate with devil's food layers; lane cake, lemon-cheese, Lady Baltimore, caramel and nut bread, and an unfrosted, not-very-sweet cake filled with chopped pecans. There were probably more because both drawers of the big old buffet were filled and a packing trunk had been moved into the dining room to have room to store the overflow.

Christmas night, supper was leftovers served cold, except for hot coffee.

The remainder of Christmas week was spent visiting and entertaining family, and by New Year's Day everybody was ready for black-eyed peas (a New Year's southern tradition) and hog jowls. Everybody also was ready to get back to work, ready to start a new year.

Now is a different day and age, but I tried to keep some of the family traditions alive so that my children, grandchildren and great-grandchildren would have something to remember.

As long as my four children and their spouses and my six grandchildren came to me at Christmas, they filled the house they grew up in. On the Sunday before Christmas, we all went back to our part of the old home place and cut a tree (a cedar, because there are no holly trees left) and put it up and decorated it. On Christmas Eve the little ones hung stockings for Santa Claus, and on Christmas Day, after Santa Claus, we passed out gifts. I always saw to it that the house felt and smelled like Christmas.

Now that I am too old to host our Christmas celebrations, I sometimes wonder if they came just to humor me, and if they would have rather stayed at their homes and watch the football games. One thing is for sure: As long as they came, I made it an old-fashioned Christmas in Georgia! ❋

The Best Christmas

By U.L. McGlinchey

Aunt Ruth had had polio as a child and had spent all but four of her 40 years on crutches. As a result, she was quite heavy from lack of exercise.

She and her aged mother, whom we called Auntie Hall and who was like an extra grandmother to us, were our next-door neighbors when my sisters and I were little. They weren't our aunts, but our custom, as in many small towns, was to call any adult who was close to you "Aunt," "Auntie" or "Uncle" instead of more formal titles.

I adored Aunt Ruth. Hardly a day passed that I didn't run up the garden path to chat with her. I never saw her in a bad mood. She was always laughing and cheerful and had a wonderful sense of humor. She taught me to sew and darn, insisting on absolute neatness and near-perfection, just like her own sewing.

Aunt Ruth was the chief operator for the telephone company in our town. She went to work every day with a wonderfully patient man who called for her in his car each morning and drove her home each night.

How I loved to go uptown to her office and watch her pull and insert the plugs attached to long cords into the switchboard when the little metal tabs fell as calls came in! She used a long stick to push the farthest tabs back up. She did all this with amazing speed and dexterity. It fascinated me, and I dreamed of becoming a telephone operator when I grew up. Alas, Aunt Ruth and her type of switchboard were long gone by that time.

Auntie Hall engaged my father in a friendly rivalry as each tried to outdo the other in growing the biggest, prettiest flowers. My father tended his flowers very carefully. Auntie Hall would wheedle a cutting from him, then simply stick it in the ground and forget about it. More often than not, her flower would flourish and outgrow its pampered parent.

Every year we invited Aunt Ruth and Auntie Hall to see our Christmas tree and share Christmas dinner. The tree was set up in the parlor on Christmas Eve after our bedtime. The decorated tree and the presents beneath it were closed off with sliding wooden doors and portieres. The doors remained closed until my father had a crackling fire going in the fireplace and Aunt Ruth and Auntie Hall had arrived to watch the delight in three little girls' eyes as my father dramatically opened them.

However, in 1925, there was a bad snow and ice storm on Christmas Eve, and it seemed impossible that Aunt Ruth and her aged mother would be able navigate even the short distance between our houses. We children were devastated at the thought of Christmas without them, but my father, a big, strong man, saved the day. He got his wheelbarrow from the cellar and went next-door.

I'll never forget the sight of a laughing Aunt Ruth as my father carried her out of her house, sat her in the wheelbarrow and tucked her crutches in beside her. Then, with little old Auntie Hall clinging to his arm, they gingerly made their way to our house. That was the best and happiest Christmas at our home for our family and our dear neighbors. ❈

A Country Christmas

By M. Elizabeth Gordon

I shall never forget the Christmas that my mother, father, brother Rich and I spent with Aunt Meg and Uncle John. I was 7 and Rich was 9.

We had often wanted to visit them, but it wasn't until a few years after the Great Depression that Father could afford to hire help to tend the animals and farm for two days.

Aunt Meg, my mother's sister, and Uncle John lived in the country. Their only companion was a huge cat named Twinkle. He never came in the house unless it rained or snowed. Then he slept on a rug in front of the coal stove.

Sometimes when it snowed there, the drifts were so deep that Aunt Meg and Uncle John were snowed in for days at a time. Rich and I could hardly wait, hoping that we would get snowed in at Christmas.

Mother always started making Christmas gifts in the summer. She knitted wool socks for Father and Uncle John. She made pot holders and gingham aprons for Aunt Meg. She made gifts for Rich and me while we slept, and they remained a mystery until Christmas morning.

Every November she ordered a bucket of candy from Sears, Roebuck and Co. There was usually a grand assortment: gumdrops, chocolate creams, toys, peanut squares, colorful ribbon candy and canes. How anxiously my brother and I waited for the postman! When the bucket finally arrived, Mother would give us each a piece before hiding the rest.

Mother also made nut fudge, peanut-butter fudge, coconut fudge and taffy. Than she spent days baking cookies shaped like stars, trees, animals and Santas. Of course, they were all decorated.

That Christmas Eve we all went to a beautiful little church about a mile from Aunt Meg's. We sang some of the old carols, including Mother's favorite, **Silent Night.**

The day before Christmas, as Mother was packing the candy, cookies and presents in boxes, Father hitched the horses to the sleigh. After giving last-minute instructions to the hired man, Mr. Lyons, we were ready to make the 7-mile trip. It was very cold and our breath made frosty designs in the air. Mother covered Rich and me with blankets and soon we were snug as bugs in a rug.

We enjoyed the ride and it didn't seem long before we arrived at Aunt Meg's. She and Uncle John were so glad to see us that Mother and Aunt Meg cried as they hugged each other. I thought they were silly; I didn't think people cried when they were happy.

After Mother and Father chatted with Aunt Meg and Uncle John for an hour or two, Aunt Meg set out the supper. Oh, the baked beans, boiled potatoes and freshly baked bread spread with butter and apple butter! For dessert we had apple pie and sugar cookies. The grown-ups drank coffee, and Rich and I had cold milk.

After we had eaten, Mother and Aunt Meg placed the presents under the untrimmed Christmas tree. That Christmas Eve we all went to a beautiful little church about a mile from Aunt Meg's. We sang some of the old carols, including Mother's favorite, *Silent Night.*

When we came out of church, it was snowing. Before we got back to Aunt Meg's, I fell asleep, and when I finally opened my eyes, it was Christmas morning.

The first thing to greet my eyes was the Christmas tree with its beautiful star on top, multicolored lights, tinfoil reflectors, colorful ornaments, tinsel and icicles. Stockings filled with candy, nuts and oranges were under the tree for Rich and me.

Our mittens were there, plus a pocketknife for Rich and a set of tin play dishes for me. Aunt Meg gave Mother a beautiful comb and Uncle John gave Father some pipe tobacco.

Mother and Aunt Meg spent all morning in the kitchen preparing the dinner. When it was finally ready, Uncle John carved the largest turkey I ever saw. To go with it there was chestnut stuffing, giblet gravy, candied sweet potatoes, mashed potatoes, peas, carrots, cranberry sauce and pickles. For dessert there was fruitcake, coconut cake, mince pie, apple pie, doughnuts and cookies.

We went to bed late that night, tired but happy.

The next morning was a sad time. As we said our goodbyes to Aunt Meg, Uncle John and Twinkle, none of us realized that we would never see Aunt Meg again. She was stricken with influenza the following spring and passed away.

I have spent many Christmases in many places, but there will never be another as enjoyable as the one we spent back on the farm with Aunt Meg and Uncle John. ✵

Two Christmases

By Susan Buckingham

Growing up in a small town in New Jersey, my two younger sisters and I were fortunate enough to celebrate two Christmases each year. There was no letdown after Dec. 25 because we knew we had another Christmas to look forward to on Jan. 7, when my Russian Orthodox father and his family celebrated Christmas.

Each Sunday after we had attended services with my dad, my mother took us to a Sunday school held in our local schoolhouse. There we celebrated Christmas with a program for which we learned pieces and songs. It was usually held the Sunday before Christmas, and we were relieved when it was over. After the program, we each received a small box filled with chocolates and hard candy.

On Christmas Eve we exchanged our gifts at home. In our childhood years, Santa came to visit, announcing his presence with the loud knock for which we had been waiting impatiently. When we opened the door, we saw our presents spread out on our porch. One year after Santa had come, our fun-loving uncle stopped in and told us Santa had dropped some gifts in the rain gutter that ran along our road. We dashed outside, and he was right! We excitedly picked up the packages and brought them into the house.

Our Jan. 7 celebration was a time for my dad's family—his father, three brothers and three sisters—to get together for church services. Some of them came from many miles away. It was a joyous time for all of us. No presents were exchanged, but we enjoyed seeing each other.

A date would be set for a group of carolers from the church to go to outlying farms and homes of members to sing Russian Christmas carols. Our aunt had taught us to sing these carols in Russian by writing down the sounds with English letters. One of my uncles was the song leader. We had great times caroling and seeing the various Christmas trees, many of which were kept in cool rooms so they would last longer. After the caroling, we were given delicious Christmas treats at each home.

Many years have passed, but I look back on those double doses of Christmas spirit with thankfulness. Our celebrations were simpler, but our hearts were filled with warm love for each other and the realization of whose birthday we were celebrating. ✱

Sweet Memories

By Jennie Hutton

Christmas is a time for remembering, so back through the portals of childhood we go. Prince and King are harnessed to the sled, ready to take us on our candy carousel.

First stop is at Aunt Merrill's. Down the winding country lane we go, up to the big brown house, sitting like a friendly puppy by the road. As the door is flung open in glad welcome, the aroma of holiday dinner mingles with the frosty air.

Inside, spun out of my tight cocoon of clothes, I eye the big polished piano with an anxious eye. It is there—the brown pottery cookie jar, plain in color and simple in design, but inside, treasure beyond belief. I hasten to climb up and reach for the …

Candy Canes

2 cups sugar
½ cup water
½ cup light corn syrup
¼ teaspoon cream of tartar
¾ teaspoon peppermint extract
1 teaspoon red food coloring

Combine sugar, water, corn syrup and cream of tartar in a heavy saucepan. Sir until sugar dissolves. Cook without stirring to soft-crack stage (270–290 degrees Fahrenheit on a candy thermometer). Remove from heat and add peppermint extract.

Divide candy into two portions. Add red food coloring to one half; set both portions of candy aside until cool enough to handle.

Pull each part separately and twist red candy around the white. Cut into lengths as desired and form into candy canes.

Dinner over, we're on our way again. We snuggle down deep until we top the hill and see Aunt Madalene's rooftop far below, blue smoke sending friendly signals.

The door is hung with green cedar boughs curled into a wreath with a big red bow and two frosted pinecones. Early dusk sends us scuttling up to the big red heater, thawing our frozen toes as we scan the groaning table—turkey, mince, apple and all the trimmings. How could we eat another bite?

Ah, but there is the Dresden Lady, full skirt hiding a dainty little candy dish.

If we stare long enough, overlooking Mama's frown and Daddy's head shake, Aunty will get up, set the lady aside, and we can help ourselves to creamy …

Dream Drops

1½ cups raisins
½ cup whole almonds
1½ cups brown sugar
½ cup light corn syrup
2 tablespoons honey
2 tablespoons water
½ cup sweetened condensed milk
¼ teaspoon salt
½ teaspoon vanilla extract
½ cup fondant

Rinse and dry raisins. Roast almonds with skins on; break kernels slightly with a rolling pin; set aside.

Combine brown sugar, corn syrup, honey and water. Add sweetened condensed milk and cook until it forms medium ball. Remove from heat. Add salt, vanilla and raisins. Add fondant and nuts; mix very thoroughly. Drop by spoonfuls onto waxed paper.

The stars are beginning to dot the purple sky. One huge one in the east reminds us of that long-ago day when a wee baby in a manger brought to the world His everlasting light of love.

Caroling along, we pull up to the white frame house set among the trees. Rustling pines whisper, "Hurry!" as we slip inside and settle ourselves down for a late-evening chat-'n'-snack with Aunt Bernice and her family.

Her kids wink knowingly and motion to the parlor. We edge slowly along … until Papa hauls us back by the ears. Scolded soundly, we

Baking With Grandma by John Slobodnik, House of White Birches nostalgia archives

bow our heads meekly, knowing full well that Cousin Arlene is opening the huge crystal bowl and filling her pinafore pockets with …

Lollipops

2 cups sugar
⅔ cup light corn syrup
1 cup water
½ teaspoon peppermint extract
½ teaspoon red food coloring

Combine sugar, corn syrup and water in a heavy saucepan and stir until sugar dissolves. Cook without stirring to hard-crack stage (300–310 degrees Fahrenheit on a candy thermometer). Wipe sugar crystals from side of pan with damp cloth. Set aside to cool. Add peppermint extract and coloring.

Lay 24 skewers 4 inches apart on greased pan. Spoon candy mixture over one end of each skewer to form 2-inch disk. Let set until hardened. Makes 2 dozen lollipops.

Another day has dawned, blush scarlet over pink. We load up the sleigh for another long day in the country. It is almost the beginning of a New Year. Holiday dining is nearly over, but Aunt Lorene insists we visit.

What a beautiful winter day! We toss snowballs back and forth, sing carols and get hungrier each wintry mile. Soon the windmill is sighted and up to the cheery little house we spin.

Inside, all is glitter and gold, the tree loaded to the topmost branch with shiny baubles. But our insides worry us more, so we go up to the table heavy with roast goose, mince and pumpkin pies, hot buns, salads and all the rest.

No one can beat Aunt Lorene in making pies, but we children can still hold more, and with a knowing wink, she ushers us into the pantry for some delicious …

Lemon Nut Balls

5 quarts popped popcorn
⅓ cup light corn syrup
2 cups sugar
½ cup water
¾ cup unsweetened pineapple juice
1 teaspoon vanilla extract
½ teaspoon lemon extract
Few drops yellow food coloring
½ cup chopped walnuts

Crisp popped corn in oven. Combine corn syrup, sugar, water and pineapple juice in a heavy saucepan. Cook without stirring to soft-crack stage (270–290 degrees Fahrenheit on a candy thermometer). Remove pan from heat and add vanilla, lemon and coloring.

Pour over popped corn, stirring gently until popcorn is evenly coated. Form into 3-inch balls and roll in chopped walnuts. Makes 2 dozen.

Late afternoon finds us on our way home, but we can't pass Aunt Madge's without stopping in. And to stop in is to eat, so we indulge with great satisfaction. Never did roast chicken and carrot cake taste so good.

Our cousins take us to the barn to see the calves, and we help with milking. Streaming jets pour into the pails in record time. We rush at feeding the cats and calves because we know what is waiting in the house when we return.

Into the cheery kitchen we spill, fighting over who will pop the corn, cook the syrup and make popcorn balls. I stand back, knowing the loser will get to help with the …

Black Walnut Taffy

3 cups brown sugar
1 tablespoon vinegar
¾ cup water
⅛ teaspoon salt
½ teaspoon vanilla extract
½ cup chopped black walnuts

Combine brown sugar, vinegar, water and salt in a heavy saucepan. Stir until sugar dissolves. Cook to soft-crack stage (270–290 degrees Fahrenheit on a candy thermometer). Remove from heat; stir in vanilla.

Pour hot candy over chopped nuts on greased platter. When partially cool, fold edges to center. When cool enough to handle, pull until light. Form into ropes; when cool, break into bite-size pieces.

A special time, a special place. What could be more so than Grandma and Grandpa's? Down the steep rocky hill we travel, up to the kitchen door. Dear, plump Grandma greets us, her blue eyes twinkling. Grandpa comes in, ruddy with cold, pitch wood piled high, and

Taffy-pulling Fun by Charles Berger, House of White Birches nostalgia archives

tells us tales while the big black stove in the corner does its duty. All those goodies—jams, pickles, hot biscuits … was there ever an end to that fabulous spread? The long ride home is a drowsy one. We drop off to sleep before the team makes the first hilltop. Daddy stands straight and tall, whistling softly as the team crunches on and on, from yesterday to today, childhood to womanhood. We clutch tightly the wonderful Christmas memories. ❋

Christmas With the Family

By Virginia Rix

The Christmases I remember best are those we celebrated in Nebraska when I was a child. My father's parents lived in the little town of Swedeburg just 2 miles from our farm. Dad's mother always wanted the family home on Christmas Eve.

My Aunt Hanna never married. She came home to take care of her parents after working for a number of years as a deaconess in settlement houses in some of the large Eastern cities at the height of the Italian and Polish immigrations in the 1920s.

Uncle Gus lived in Omaha and worked for a law firm. Later he married a schoolteacher whose widowed mother lived with them. They never had children, so my sister and I were the only children in the family. We all went to Grandma and Grandpa's on Christmas Eve for as long as we lived in Nebraska.

When we arrived at Grandma and Grandpa's, we left our wraps on the bed in their downstairs bedroom. On a small table in the northeast corner of that room, we always found two bowls of rice pudding, set there to cool. It was made by slowly cooking the rice in milk with a cinnamon stick on the back of the old iron cookstove. It had to be stirred often to keep it from scorching, but it made the fluffiest of rice pudding, not like the kind people make today. Sugar was added and the pudding was poured into bowls. Then the top of the pudding was decorated with a lattice of ground cinnamon with a raisin in the middle of each square.

One year after I was out of high school, I found a nut in my pudding. There had never been nuts in the pudding before, so I mentioned it. My aunt and grandmother pretended to be very surprised and said that it meant that I would be the next one married—an old custom. I always suspected that they slipped that nut-meat into my pudding and that it didn't just turn up by chance.

Being Swedish, we always had the traditional "white Christmas" dinner—huge, steaming platters of *lutefisk* (a Scandinavian codfish dish), bowls of boiled white potatoes and milk gravy, and the rice pudding for dessert. The only things not white were hot mustard and lingonberries. My dad and his brother could put away plate after plate of fish and potatoes covered with gravy and drizzled with hot mustard.

I don't know how traditional it was, but Grandma always served another meat dish for those who didn't like lutefisk. Sometimes it was Swedish meatballs, or a small beef roast or roast chicken with brown gravy. I always appreciated this, as it took me years of having a small piece of lutefisk every Christmas before I learned to like it.

After everyone was full, the double doors to the parlor were opened and there, in the corner, was the Christmas tree alight with candles—a thrilling sight for a small child.

I vividly remember the last year we had lighted candles on the Christmas tree. As my aunt reached behind the tree to get a toy washing machine for me, her hair caught fire. My uncle was sitting on the piano stool near the tree. He whirled toward her and swept both hands up each side of her head and just "swooshed" the fire out. It all happened so fast that no one was hurt, but it could have been a tragedy. After that we never had lighted candles on our Christmas trees. Many years later we had electricity and strings of lights, but I can still remember how pretty the candles were, and the mingled scents of evergreen and candle wax.

For many years our little country church had its Christmas program on Christmas Eve. After dinner, we all went over to the church for the program. The Christmas program was the highlight of the year for us children. We always had new dresses, learned poems, and practiced songs and tableaux. The smaller children often had just a line or two—and several went up on the platform together and recited in turn. One year, to the amusement of everyone except her parents, one little girl poked her finger into the middle of her dress and wound it up until her panties were showing.

Our Santa Claus was not the jolly, fat, red-suited person we see today, but an old-fashioned St. Nicholas in a long fur coat and fur cap. Some of the little children were frightened and cried. After the program, each child always got a big, shiny, red Delicious apple, an orange and a bag of hard candies with pretty designs in the centers.

Mother's family lived 600 miles away, in Denver, so they sent their gifts by mail. Of course, Santa had come during the night and left gifts for us to find on Christmas morning. We also opened the gifts from Denver then, as well as the presents from a friend of Mother's who lived at Fort Morgan. She always sent the most beautiful books, which I enjoyed since I loved to read.

When we were small, Mother made Santa Claus very real for us. We always left a plate of cookies and some cocoa for Santa and sugar cubes for his reindeer on the kitchen table before we went to bed. We knew he had been there because the next morning, the cup had been used and most of the cookies and sugar cubes were gone. Proof enough!

When I was about 8, I had a furious argument with a schoolmate who tried to tell me there was no Santa Claus. The first year that Mother told me my schoolmate was right was the loneliest I remember. My little sister still believed and I felt so lost. It took several years for me to recover and capture the true spirit of Christmas. I resolved never to let that happen to a child of mine.

When the Depression came, we made do. We cut our own trees on the farm. We made many of our decorations, too. Of course we always strung popcorn and cranberries, but we also carefully saved the tinfoil from our Hershey bars for making ornaments. And we removed the tinsel "icicles" each year to save for the next year instead of throwing them out with the tree as people do these days.

One year we made a house pet of one of our kittens. One night shortly before Christmas, in the middle of the night, we were awakened by a loud crash in the living room. Apparently the moonlight shining on the tree had tantalized the kitten, and it made a flying leap off the foot of the studio couch and landed in the middle of the tree. What a mess!

There were few store-bought gifts in those days, except those we received from Uncle Gus. My sister's birthday and mine both fall during the first few days of January. Our uncle, who was quite a tease, said he guessed he would have to combine our Christmas and birthday presents. We naturally took a dim view of this. After all, if our birthdays had been in the summer, we would get birthday presents, too.

I vividly remember the last year we had lighted candles on the Christmas tree. As my aunt reached behind the tree to get a toy washing machine for me, her hair caught fire.

We always made long wish lists for Uncle Gus. One year my sister put a Santa Claus on her list. She was still quite small and had a sweet tooth. She really wanted a chocolate Santa, but poor Uncle Gus didn't understand and got a cardboard stand-up Santa. Sis was disappointed, of course, but her Santa was the same size as a St. Nicholas figure that had been given to our mother when she was child. From that year on, the two were placed at either end on top of the piano. I don't know what became of the Santa since then, but I still have St. Nicholas.

One year my mother's brother and his family drove out from Denver to spend Christmas with us. Their children were both years younger than my sister and I, and Shirley, their youngest, was just at the age when she had decided there was no Santa Claus. As we were getting ready to retire for the evening, everyone told Shirley she'd better go to bed so Santa could come. But she was skeptical and kept balking.

Mother slipped out of the room unnoticed and went up to the attic, where we had some sleigh bells that Dad's family had brought from Sweden. Mother gently shook the bells; then, a short time later, she shook them again, a little harder. Shirley stopped dead still. Her eyes as big as saucers, she turned and made a beeline for her bed and pulled the covers over her head. When we all followed her, she pulled the covers down and begged, "Tell him I'm asleep! Tell him I'm asleep!" For one more year, she believed. I've often wondered how she felt when she finally found out the truth.

Remembering my lonely feeling when I "lost" Santa Claus, I made sure that our son, when he was small, understood why we celebrate Christmas. He knew early the story of our Savior's birth and was always reminded that it was Jesus' birthday we were celebrating.

There is no way to avoid Santa Claus and it's difficult to explain to a very small child, so we had all the fun we could with that myth. But I will never forget the satisfaction I felt one year, after he was in school, when my son came to me shortly before Christmas and asked, "Mom, can we play the Santa Claus game this year?" I was elated that I had helped him enjoy Santa Claus without losing sight of the real reason we celebrate Christmas. He knew it was a game, but even though he was getting to be a big boy, he wasn't ready to give up his Christmas stocking.

I remember my father telling me about Christmas in Sweden when he was a boy, and attending midnight services in the church in their small town. He said there were two huge evergreen trees, one on each side of the altar, and both were alight with candles. He said that all those flickering candles made the whole church glitter. His description was so vivid that I could almost see it myself. We will never see such sights again, except with our mind's eye. What a wonderful thing is memory! ✻

A Christmas To Remember

By Doris Monson Heino

*I*t was September 1924. Dad and Mother took Alice, who was to be my roommate, and me to the university. I was only 16 and Mother had many misgivings about me going so far away. What if I got homesick? But I had no intention of getting homesick; I had been looking forward to going to school for six years.

We left in high spirits at 6 a.m. In those days before "hard roads," a trip of 150 miles in an Overland car was a big undertaking. We arrived at the university late that afternoon.

When my folks left for home early the next morning, Mother was still tearful, bemoaning the fact that she was leaving me in such a large, frightening place. After all, I had been raised on a farm and had graduated from a high school of just 55 pupils.

All that fall I looked forward to going home for Christmas and impressing my family with my thoughtful gifts. I considered many presents for my sister and brothers, but discarded them for other ideas. I wanted this to be a really impressive holiday!

I finally decided to take a pair of lovebirds to my mother. (She had had a pair of birds several years earlier, but Aledo and Viola had died and been properly buried in the apple orchard in Dr. Blosser cigarette boxes.) Then I saw a pretty umbrella and decided it would be a good gift for my young sister. A small black-and-white ceramic teapot with four cups seemed to be a good gift for my grandmother, who liked her tea. I found other gifts for Dad and my brothers.

I wasn't thinking about riding the train home, nor did I anticipate the severe ice storm that hit the week before Christmas. The birds were to make the trip in their bamboo cage, which was wrapped in newspapers and then enclosed in several sacks for insulation. I packed most of the other gifts in my suitcase, but I had to carry the umbrella.

A cab took Alice and me to the station. As our train carried us homeward, we noticed that the telegraph wires along the tracks were broken in many places and hanging low, weighed down with ice.

When we reached our destination, I was still 3 miles from home and Dad wasn't there to meet me. It was frosty cold and snowing and I was wondering what on earth to do. I couldn't walk home with all of my bundles. But Alice's brother had come to meet her, and taking pity on me, he offered to take me home in his bobsled.

I didn't realize how severe the storm had been until I saw the downed telephone lines and the snowdrifts that blocked the roads in many places. The air was so cold and crisp that my nose hurt when I breathed. When I finally got home, I learned that Dad hadn't come to meet me because he had heard that the trains were not running because of the storm.

I was so thankful to see everyone and to be inside my own home again. Mother had covered the newel post in the hall with white crepe paper and had decorated it to look like a snowman. A big tree stood in the bay window. The little puppy my older brother had given my younger brother was tearing around excitedly, and the birds I brought for Mother began to chirp as soon as they were unwrapped.

It was truly a Christmas to remember! ❋

A Sweet Reunion

By J.B. Cearley

I was 9 years old the last of November. Soon after my birthday, my parents began talking about inviting company to visit us for Christmas. "Why don't we write to all our relatives and tell them we want them to come to a family reunion at Christmas?" Daddy said to Mother. "If we invite everyone, then enough will show up to have a good time together. We might have 20—maybe more."

That next week, Mother wrote a stack of letters and Big Brother and I carried them to our rural mailbox. We lived a little over 3 miles west of Bridgeport, Texas. Dad was in shares farming my Grandma Cearley's land. We had over 200 acres and a lot of cattle, plus a small herd of Jersey dairy cows.

A week before Christmas, I had to help Mother with the plans for the Christmas reunion. Mother planned to make a variety of candies. Each night after supper, I cracked those hard, black walnuts, placing the nuts on a sledgehammer hitting them with the claw hammer. I used a sharp, small knife to pick the nutmeats from the hard shells.

Next were the pecans. They had much thinner shells than those ironlike black walnuts, and I had to be careful not to smash them. Getting a quart of nice, whole pecan halves took me only two evenings.

A week before Christmas, Mother bought the other ingredients she needed for the candy, and four days before Christmas, she began to make it. She mixed the ingredients in a large bowl and then spread the mixture in two large cooking pans. Then she added the walnuts I had labored over. Later she removed two long pans of candy from the oven.

Lunchtime finally arrived, and I had to wait until I had eaten my beans and corn bread before I could sample that candy. I still think

that it was the best candy I have ever tasted. I wanted to get that bowl of candy and hide it from the relatives—I felt I deserved it more than the ones I had met.

That afternoon Mother had me and my older brother help her make two big pans of chocolate candy that she called fudge. I began to think we would have enough candy to feed everyone in the county.

Two days before we expected the relatives, Mother made a white layer cake, with icing spread all over the top and sides. Then she covered the top of the cake with pecan halves arranged in rings. She also made a devil's food cake and covered it with chocolate icing. Mother was some cook!

When Dad looked at the huge table overflowing with cakes and candy, he chuckled and said, "If any relatives come, they'll all get fat on these goodies. If no one comes, we'll eat 'til we pop!"

They came! My Uncle Hub Stroud, husband of Dad's youngest sister, arrived soon after sunup on Christmas Eve in his old Star touring car. He brought his wife and three boys. The moment he climbed down from that old Star, he shook hands with Daddy and said, "I came early to help you butcher a hog."

Dad told him, "Well, let's get busy and get it done."

My Aunt Jewel got out of the rickety Star and carried a box of food into the house. I knew we wouldn't starve if the relatives helped out with the food.

We got busy with the butchering. Brother and I built a roaring fire under the big wash pot and filled it with water from our well. Dad and Uncle Hub got a pig from the pen and killed it. I helped pour hot water over the animal so it would be easier to remove the hair with butcher-knife scrapers. A few minutes later, Daddy hung the animal from a tree limb using our wire stretchers and we were ready to cut up the meat.

The hams, shoulders, slab bacon, pork loins and sausage meat were placed on the wagon, which I had washed with scalding water from the big iron pot. I turned the crank on the sausage grinder and Daddy mixed the seasonings with the meat as it was ground, then we packed it into cloth bags my mother had made. Then Dad seasoned the hams, shoulders, ribs and sides of bacon and placed them in a barrel for curing.

For lunch that day we had fresh pork chops, beans, homemade hominy, stewed potatoes and carrots from our garden, topped off with some of my aunt's cake.

Late on Christmas Eve, two more cars of relatives arrived at the old farmstead. I began to think that we might have a crowd. My parents were elated to see kinfolk they had not heard from in three years. I had never seen so much hugging, hand-shaking and backslapping in my nine years. Unfortunately, I came in for a lot of hugging and kissing by old aunts until I thought I needed to wash my face.

I figured we had close to 30 people, counting Grandma and our own family of six. Brother and I and all the cousins had to sleep on pallets on the floor that night.

We awoke early Christmas morning when Daddy built a roaring fire in the rock fireplace. Mother soon called for us to hurry and see what Santa Claus had brought.

It didn't take us long to dress. We hurried into the room with the fireplace to see toys everywhere. Santa had brought me the race car I wanted, a beautiful automobile painted bright red. I also got warm socks, gloves and long-handled underwear. Santa also gave me an assortment of sparklers, firecrackers and Roman candles.

By the time we had finished our biscuits, gravy, bacon, scrambled eggs, jam, cereal, milk and coffee, I heard a racket approaching our yard. I hurried out and there was the first Chevrolet I had ever seen, bouncing along the roadway. When it stopped at our gate, Dad walked up, took a look at the touring car and said, "Well, I'll be! You folks light and we'll visit a spell."

It was my Uncle Forrest Cearley and his family. They had left their farm home near Iowa Park in north central Texas soon after midnight to drive to our place for the reunion. Again, I got a shower of kisses from my aunt.

Later that morning, two of Mother's sisters and their families arrived in Model T's for the family get-together. Everyone was happy because we had never had so many families together before.

Since we were farm folks, we had to do the milking and tend to our regular chores. I got my milk bucket and hurried to the milking barn. When I opened the door and entered the barn to get feed for the cows, I saw our old cat, Fluffy, get up from her bed on a bale of hay and meow to me. When she didn't offer to come down as usual, I climbed up on the bales of hay. And did I get a Christmas surprise! Fluffy had five black-and-white baby kittens!

When Big Brother and I were free to play, I taught our city cousins how much fun we could have by climbing to the top of our tall haystack and sliding down. Some of them had never been on a farm and were unaware of the fun country kids could have.

Soon Daddy called the older boys to help him set up a table for the youngsters on the porch. Our two wooden sawhorses and three long, 1- x 12-inch boards made an excellent table for 20 kids. We set long boards across 5-gallon buckets to make benches to sit on while we ate.

The women had placed all the food on the long buffet in the dining room. We were to heap our plates and then find a place at the table.

I got my plate and thought I might take a little of everything, but that was impossible. There was baked ham, fried chicken, turkey and dressing, beef roast, sausage, ribs and fish, corn, pinto beans, carrots, black-eyed peas, fried potatoes, lima beans, potato salad, onions and pea salads. There was hot homemade bread, corn bread, muffins, biscuits and oat-barley bread. Dessert offered a choice of seven cakes, coconut pie, chocolate pie, lemon cream pie, apricot pie, apple pie and fruit salad. I counted nine kinds of candy. I haven't been exposed to such a feast since that day.

After we had eaten our Christmas dinner and the food was put away, Uncle Forrest read the Christmas story as found in the second chapter of the Gospel of Luke from

Great-grandpa Cearley's big Bible. Then we had a prayer by three of the men and sang carols, ending with *Silent Night*.

Daddy walked down to the barn and corral to see about our mare that was due to foal soon. He returned in a few minutes and told me and Brother to go to the corral and see what was there for us.

Another Christmas surprise! Our mare had given birth to the prettiest paint colt with brown and black spots all over his white coat. He was standing by his mother, nursing. Brother and I climbed over the fence to pet the beautiful colt.

Dad walked over to where we were admiring the foal. After a minute he said, "I want you boys to take good care of your pony."

So it was *our* pony! We were so excited about that paint colt that we were beside ourselves. We never dreamed that the folks would give us the colt. We began making plans for riding it and for hitching him to a cart when he was old enough. What a wonderful Christmas we were having!

Late that afternoon, we had to say goodbye to our many relatives. Those who had jobs in town had to get back to work. The farmers had to return home to care for their livestock.

As the last relative waved goodbye and drove away, Daddy turned to Mother and said, "Well, we had a nice reunion."

"Yes," she agreed. "This was probably the best reunion and Christmas that we will have for a long time. I did so enjoy seeing so many of our folks."

It was truly a wonderful Christmas—the kind all folks should have at every opportunity. I still love to remember that wonderful Christmas more than 60 years later. ✳

Gifts of the Heart

Chapter Two

For a long time I really envied my Grandma and Grandpa Tate. Each Christmas when we journeyed the 3 or 4 miles to their home, I always found the last part of the gravel country lane leading down to the house lined with cars full of children and grandchildren who had come to see them on that special day.

Grandma and Grandpa had 11 children who lived into adulthood. Most of those children had large families of their own, and each made the pilgrimage at Yuletide to the little four-room house to show their love and honor toward the patriarch and matriarch of the family.

Some of my cousins were already grown and had families of their own. By the time Grandma and Grandpa's children, grandchildren, great-grandchildren and the "in-laws" were included, there must have been over 100 people show up on Christmas. We tried to come in shifts to control the crowding, but several families—including ours—had no telephone, so invariably it seemed as though we kids had to stay outside in the frosty December air to make room in the house for the adults and the smallest children.

We were summoned inside only when it was time for us to give Grandma and Grandpa the Christmas presents we had bought or made for them. There, in the warmth of the tiny living room, they were holding court for the day. They were surrounded by dozens and dozens of gifts from as many progeny. I was amazed and, as I said, a little envious of anyone who received so many gifts each year.

With a little gentle coaxing from Daddy, I shyly walked up with some little something for each of them. I had saved pennies throughout the year and I used several on my Grandma and Grandpa Tate's gifts.

After they pulled open the primitive wrapping and made sufficient "oohs" and "aahs" over whatever trinket I had selected, Grandpa reached down into a basket, rummaged around for a few seconds and pulled out a thin package marked "Kenneth." It was usually a handkerchief—one, not a package of three. Then it was, "Thank you," followed by a big bear hug from each of my grandparents and a muffled, "I love you!" I moved back outside to make room for the next gift-bearer.

Years later I realized the silliness of my envy. Most of the gifts we children brought were useless to Grandma and Grandpa. Yet there was always something in that basket—despite lean years—that had my name on it. How they afforded even the simplest things, I will never know.

But one thing I do know. Christmas at Grandma and Grandpa's house was filled with enough love to make the hard times pale in its glow, at least for a few days. That is the most important lesson in giving—and receiving—gifts of the heart in those Good Old Days gone by.

—*Ken Tate*

Holiday Cabin by Sam Timm, courtesy of Wild Wing Inc.

Dolls From the Christmas Trunk

By Eleanor Vance Koren

In the early 1920s, Aunt Ella, Mama's only sister, always paid us a visit around Christmas. She wasn't married yet, so Mama's three little girls and one boy took the place of her own at that time.

How Papa complained when they received her letter telling when her train would arrive at the town depot! He said, "I sure hope she doesn't bring that old trunk with her again. I hurt my back last time getting it up that stairway to her room. Did you tell her about that, Lucy?"

We all looked at Mama, afraid she had told Aunt Ella not to fill it so full if she brought it. Even though our hired man, Jay, always helped Papa carry it in, it still was a strain on both men. On the appointed day, at the appointed hour, all three of us girls pressed our faces close to the window when they returned from the depot, straining to see if the old trunk was in the back of the wagon.

Then Aunt Ella bustled in, all smiles, with a cheery greeting. She hugged each of us and exclaimed over how we had grown. She wore long dresses and coats, with fur wrapped around her shoulders. A pretty hat perched on top of her heavy black hair, which she wore in a pompadour style held up by large celluloid hairpins with few pretty curved combs tucked around it. Aunt Ella was the head waitress in a large hotel in a large city and always dressed in the latest style.

As soon as the horses were put away for the night, we heard Jay and Papa struggling with the old trunk. Papa was cursing in low tones and Mama had a happy but worried look on her face. But Aunt Ella never seemed to mind Papa.

Mama waited supper in the old range stove, so as soon as the trunk was safely upstairs, we sat down to eat. Aunt Ella amused us with stories of the big city and the hotel where she worked. She talked with an Irish brogue. Her father had come from Ireland and had raised Aunt Ella and several brothers after their mother died. My mother had been raised by another family; she had been very little when her mother died, and her father felt she needed a woman's care. The people who raised her must have taught her to speak the way they did, because she didn't have the Irish brogue like her brothers and sister.

Mama and Aunt Ella sat up late after the rest of us were in bed, talking and laughing while they sipped tea. It seemed they were trying to make up for the lost years together they had missed growing up.

The next morning, after the dishes were done and Papa and Jay were out in the barn doing chores, we all sat around and waited for Aunt Ella to suggest opening her trunk. When she noticed our anxious faces, she said, "Well now, let's go upstairs and open my trunk because we might just find something in it for each of you darlin's."

It was hard not to scramble upstairs ahead of Mama and Aunt Ella, but we knew we shouldn't enter her room without her asking us in. After we were inside, we sat on the side of the bed, all excited, and waited for the lid of the magic trunk to be opened.

There was something pretty for Mama on top. She exclaimed, "Oh, Ella, you shouldn't spend your hard-earned money on us!"

Aunt Ella answered, "Sure and begorra, if I can't spend some of it on my favorite family, what good is it?"

We appreciated those presents so much! The only other gifts we received during the year were a homemade dress for our birthday and another for Christmas, plus a doll from Santa and a stocking full of nuts and candy.

The most memorable Christmas was when Aunt Ella wrote to my mother and told her not to buy dolls for us for Christmas because she had already bought us some. We received those beautiful dolls under the tree on Christmas morning. I loved my doll so much that I carried it around with me most of the time. Christmas for me was a doll; without one my Christmas would have been very disappointing, no matter what else I received.

A few nights after Christmas, my folks had to make a trip into town and Aunt Ella stayed with us. My younger sister and I were giving our dolls a ride around the table when our dolls' heads crashed together. My doll's head broke into several pieces and instantly, my whole world crumbled.

When Aunt Ella saw how devastated I was, she took me by the hand and walked me upstairs. I thought she was going to get me ready for bed, but she took me to her room and opened her trunk. She reached way down in the bottom and pulled out another doll. It wasn't as pretty as the first one, but I clutched it to my chest and looked up at her like she was a fairy godmother. She told my mother later that I looked up at her with such an adoring look that it made her feel like a fairy godmother, and it really made her Christmas that year.

A few years later I heard that she had bought three dolls for us girls and then saw three more much prettier ones on sale, so she put the first ones in the bottom of her trunk for her brother's girls, whom she would be visiting after leaving our house. When I broke mine, she couldn't stand the heartbreak in my eyes, so she decided to give me another one. From that night on, there was always a special bond between Aunt Ella and me.

Years later, when she was in her 60s as I am now, she asked me if I remembered the night when I broke my doll and she found another one for me in her old trunk. I said, "Yes, I remember it very clearly. It was one of the happiest Christmases I ever had, and I think I have loved that old trunk and you ever since." ❉

The Yellow Christmas Boxes

By Kathryn Patterson

My parents were married in 1913. By the time they had been married 10 years, they had seven children—first, four sons; then I came along in September 1921; and two years later, the twins were born, a boy and a girl.

My father was a farmer so there was always food to put on the table. We always had plenty of milk, cream, butter, eggs and meat. Each year my father butchered a pig and a cow. My mother canned the beef, quarts and quarts of it. The hams were smoked in a smokehouse. Mother fried down the remaining pork, put it in 20-gallon stone crocks, and then covered it with melted lard. The lard hardened, preserving the fried meat. The crocks were stored in the cool cellar where the lard always stayed firm.

My mother always had a large garden, too. It provided our vegetables summer and winter because she canned whatever we didn't eat fresh.

We all went to a country school with all eight grades in one room. I was already in school when the Depression hit. But the Depression didn't seem unusual to me; when you come from a family as large as ours, there was always a "depression," it seemed.

Although we had plenty to eat, there was never anything fancy or grand. Our mother kept our nine-room farmhouse clean. Our furniture included only the most essential things—beds, chests, a dresser or two, a large dining-room table, odds and ends of chairs, and a big, old, black, wood-burning kitchen range.

When Christmas came around each year we each got one gift or toy. That's where the yellow boxes came in.

Each year, shortly before Christmas, my mother would go to the shoe shop in our small town and get seven empty shoe boxes. The owner of the shoe store must have known she'd be coming because he always had the boxes for her. The boxes must have held men's new work shoes, as they were quite wide and always yellow. All seven boxes were always the exact same size and color.

My mother must have started making homemade Christmas candy a few weeks before Christmas. And she must have done it while we were at school or after we went to bed, because I never saw any candy until Christmas Eve. She surely hid it well, because even with seven children running around the house, none of us ever found it. But then, our parents kept us so busy that we didn't have time to look for it anyway.

Santa Claus always came about 9 p.m. on Christmas Eve, after the milking and farm chores were done. Santa Claus would give each of us our one present apiece and leave. Then our mother would give each of us our own big, yellow box. Each of the seven boxes was packed exactly alike. There was a big red apple, an orange and some Christmas mixed nuts filling about one-third of the box. The rest of it was filled with all kinds of Mother's wonderful, homemade Christmas candy—chocolate fudge, chocolate-covered bonbons, and my favorite candy of all, sea foam. It is still my favorite homemade candy and I make it each Christmas for my family to enjoy. They love it, too.

We then had to keep our boxes in our bedrooms or in some other hiding place. Believe me, we watched our boxes like hawks. We counted the pieces of candy, and if one or two were missing, we knew someone had gotten into it. I speak from experience here; I remember taking a piece or two here and there from my brothers' boxes when I had to make their beds or clean their rooms.

In 1933, another daughter was born. Soon she too would receive a yellow shoe box filled with goodies. I was about 5 years old when I first got my own box, and I got a yellow box every year until I was 19 and ready to be married.

I now make all the same candies at Christmastime that my mother made. I keep my homemade candies in covered pails, and each day I put several pieces of each kind on a tray and set it out for whoever wants to eat it.

And every December when I am making homemade candy for my children and grandchildren, I recall those Good Old Days with the yellow boxes that came on Christmas Eve. ❄

The Christmas Hat

By Evelyn Lyon

"I know that's what they are giving me for Christmas," Aunt Nora excitedly confided to Mother one day a few weeks before Christmas. "I *know* it is, for it disappeared from stock, and I *know* it hasn't been sold."

Aunt Nora was Mother's spinster sister who spent weekends with us and worked at a millinery shop in a nearby town. When the winter merchandise had come in that year, she had unpacked it. She had fallen in love with "the hat" as soon as she saw it. But it was far too expensive for her meager purse. The clerks were allowed to buy merchandise at cost, but even so, in the mid-1920s, $2.98 was an unheard-of price to pay for a hat.

It was a gorgeous thing nonetheless, a soft velvet cloche with a tiny brim, all in muted, variegated shades of wine and rose with just a touch of light emerald green. Every seam was bound with shimmering, wine-colored satin, and a tiny, perky bow peeped out from under the brim on the left side. No wonder she fell in love with it!

From that day until Christmas, Aunt Nora endured an emotional tug of war! One day she would make up her mind that the hat had been sold without her knowing about it; then she would sink into the depths of despair. But the next day her spirits would rally, and she was sure they had taken it out of stock to give to her for a Christmas gift. Her employers, two spinster ladies who owned the shop, knew how much she longed for the hat.

Of course, Mother knew the secret also, for one day when she was in the shop and Aunt Nora was out on an errand, Miss Maude gave Mother the hat, all wrapped and ready for Christmas. Mother was to take it home and hide it from Aunt Nora.

However, Mother made one miserable mistake! She told Dad and two of my uncles about the hat, and practical jokers that they were, it was too good of an opportunity to let pass. So they spirited the hat away without anyone, including Mother, knowing about their devious plot.

Christmas that year was to be celebrated at Aunt Ida Bailey's house. When Aunt Nora arrived on Christmas morning, sure enough, under the tree in the little parlor was a package just the shape of a hat box. It was wrapped in pretty holly paper and tied with a soft ribbon bow. The card read, "To Miss Nora, Merry Christmas from Miss Maude and Miss Zula." Aunt Nora's excitement knew no bounds! In fact, the laughter and excitement ran extremely high that year with *everyone*—especially with Dad and my two uncles.

Then came the most exciting time of all, opening the packages! Aunt Ida's parlor was very small and seldom used—just for weddings, funerals and Christmas trees. Since there was no electricity, there were real candles on the tree, and all precautions were taken against fire. We were seated systematically, with Dad and my uncles at strategic points with pans of water at hand in case of fire.

Then Aunt Ida lit the candles, one by one. What an enchanting, breathtaking moment! We watched with awe as the little candles scattered among the homemade tree decorations gave off a soft glow.

We all were very still for just a moment, taking in all of its magical beauty. Then one by one, Aunt Ida blew out the candles and we distributed the gifts. Everyone, including the children, was looking forward to Aunt Nora's Christmas hat. After all, it was all we had heard about since Thanksgiving!

Needless to say, Aunt Nora's gift was the first to be opened. When Uncle John handed her the package, a strange quiet came over the entire room. Her hands trembled and her chin quivered as the paper rattled and the lid came slowly off the hat box.

Window Shopping by Ron Delli Colli, House of White Birches nostaliga archives

There, in a nest of white tissue paper—and then Aunt Nora screamed! She slammed the lid back on the box and quickly surveyed the room. Then she took one more peek into the box, and dissolved into tears and laughter.

My dad and uncles were hysterical! One bald, rotund uncle literally rolled on the floor with laughter. The room was complete bedlam, all the other gifts forgotten.

Above shouts of laughter we could hear, "Let's see it, Nora!"

"Try it on, Nora!"

"Let me wear it, Nora!"

Finally Aunt Nora gained control of herself enough to take it out of the box. Instead of the lovely velvet hat, she held up the most horrible, dilapidated, old, blue felt hat that had belonged to my mother years earlier. My uncles and Dad had "decorated" it! In the center of the crown was one old, faded, red paper rose. Old flowers, ribbons and junk covered the wide, floppy brim. A red onion,dry top and all, hung rakishly over the left eye, while at the same angle over the right eye hung a mouse trap holding a rubber mouse.

Aunt Nora began to beg for the real Christmas gift—the real hat. But they insisted that this was the one. By now, the hat was making the rounds, and each uncle took a turn wearing it.

It was not until the last gift was unwrapped and opened that Aunt Nora was allowed to have her lovely, new, velvet hat. And it really was a beautiful creation!

This story joined the annals of other family jokes and was told so many times at other Christmases that it almost became a legend. ❄

Santa Looked a Lot Like Dad

By Ward Cummines

As I lay at the foot of my bed with the pillow scrunched up under my chest, I gazed out the window and watched the snowflakes lazily slipping from side to side, descending unhurriedly to the vast, cottonlike blanket that covered and softened the harsh angles of progress. From somewhere below came the sounds of carolers as they, with voices blended in harmony, sang of the little drummer boy:

Come, they told me, pa rum pum pum pum,
A newborn King to see, pa rum pum
pum pum. …

I listened, captivated by this beautiful song. Sleep was out of the question.

The carolers moved on and I began to speculate as to how long it would be until I could get out of bed—until I could prove to myself that all the wonderful things I had been told about Christmas were really true. I wanted to see the Christmas tree with the bright, shiny balls of different reflective colors, with red-striped candy canes and tinfoil icicles, and with a gold and white angel perched on the very top. I wanted to see the Christ child in the manger, with Mary and Joseph praying, with the three wise men bearing gifts of frankincense and myrrh. I wanted to see the sheep and the cows bowing in reverence in the presence of Jesus. And, of course, being a little boy, I wanted to see the toys.

Suddenly and faintly, a long way off, I heard the jingling of sleigh bells. They seemed to be heading toward our house. I assumed they were on the roof. I listened intently, and as I did, the words of Clement C. Moore lilted through my head:

When what to my wondering eyes should appear,
But a miniature sleigh and eight tiny reindeer.
Could it be possible? I thought. *Could they be sleigh bells? Could they be Santa's sleigh bells?*

My speculations were suddenly disrupted by a loud knock at the front door, followed by a deep and resonating, "Ho, ho, ho!"

Without thinking of this digression from Clement Moore's poem, I flew to the top of the stairs and peeked between the risers. From this perch, I was able to see the glistening black shine of a patent-leather boot. Moving down two more steps, my eyes widened. There, just below me, in his beautiful red velvet suit, was Santa himself.

After getting over the initial shock, I was further surprised by the position of his left arm—wrapped snugly around my mother's waist. I shifted my weight to get a better view and the stair squeaked.

Quickly my mother looked in my direction and then whispered something in Santa's ear.

"Edward," she called, "get your brother and come on down. I want you to meet someone."

Needless to say, I responded to her request immediately. My brother, deep in sleep, was difficult to arouse until I mentioned the magical word: "Santa." He then slid out of bed, and after straightening the twisted boot of his flannel sleepers, toddled along after me as we headed toward the staircase.

Downstairs Mother introduced us to the venerable gentleman. She had a twinkle in her voice as she spoke. It was the kind of voice that makes you pause and think—the kind of voice that implies, "I know something you don't know."

After the introductions, Santa took my brother, Buddy, up onto his lap. Though I hadn't been deliberately scrutinizing him, I felt an aura of familiarity—a charisma I couldn't explain. I stared at him as he asked the question, which, during many subsequent visits on Santa's lap, I have heard many times: "Have you been a good boy?"

That kind of question sure puts a guy on the spot. If you say "Yes" to Santa who, we been cautioned, "knew our innermost thoughts," where would we stand? We would get coal in our stockings. If, on the other hand, we said

"No"—well, I wouldn't even contemplate the result of that.

Finally, Santa was able to drag a weak and barely audible "Yes" from Buddy.

But then Santa asked him, "What would you like for Christmas?" And the change in my brother was startling. His reticence and shyness immediately were transformed into garrulous loquacity. If there was a toy that my kid brother failed to request, it was only because it was not yet on the market. His requests ranged from a blackboard with chalk to a paddleball, from a xylophone to ball-bearing roller skates—the kind with a skate key, no less.

While waiting my turn, my attention was briefly diverted by a familiar smell, the odor of William's after-shave. I looked behind me for Dad, who normally was the bearer of this pleasant aroma, but he was not there.

I didn't give it too much thought, for I was by then heading for Santa, who was now beckoning to me. As he waited for me, he drummed his fingernails on the wooden trim of the overstuffed couch. Again I felt the twinge of familiarity, especially after noticing that Santa's onyx ring, with the big "E" on its face, was just like Dad's.

After being deposited on his lap, I, too, was asked the inevitable questions. I immediately replied "Yes" to the first question in order to get speedily to the second.

"I want a Railway Express truck, an' a scooter, an' a Number 3 erector set."

Santa contemplated what I supposed to be a reasonable request and gave me a squeeze—again, strangely familiar. But I could not figure out why it seemed familiar. The voice was deeper than the one I was thinking of, but still—Santa's eyes and nose, and the small scar on the upper lip, visible under a strange floating mustache, were all pounding on the door of my memory.

Trying to go to sleep that night was quite a chore. When Mom and Dad dropped in for a good-night kiss, I was tickled by a small piece of cotton that had somehow stuck to Dad's face. Suddenly it all became clear—the voice, the scar and the strand of auburn hair out of place among all that white. Now I knew why Santa wore a ring with an "E." The "E" was for "Edward," just like my name—and just like Dad's. Santa looked a lot like Dad because Santa *was* Dad.

Instead of being disappointed, however, I was elated. I was at the age when I was beginning to require more detailed explanations about some things—things like how reindeer can fly, or how a 250-pound elf can negotiate the confines of a 6-inch chimney flue.

It had all been so confusing. We had been with Mom when she returned a defective toy—but to Gimbel's or Macy's or Penney's instead of Santa's North Pole workshop.

And we had observed that Santa suffered a constant glandular battle. In the three or four weeks prior to his big day, we found him alternately gaining and losing weight. Sometimes his mustache curled up, sometimes down. His voice varied widely, and he'd had blue eyes at Macy's on Tuesday and brown at Gimbel's on Wednesday. He'd spoken to us with Harvard eloquence one time and Brooklyn provincialism the next.

But his most amazing feat was his ability to change the color of his skin. We kids had seen him as white, black, yellow, red, pink, tan, wrinkled, not so wrinkled and not at all wrinkled.

Considering all these inconsistencies, is it any wonder that we kids began to question? Is it any wonder that we searched for other answers? Is it any wonder that I was deeply relieved—and pleasantly surprised—to find that Santa looked so much like Dad because, instead of being a fairy-tale stranger, he was in fact a real live person much closer to my heart? ❋

Christmas On 48 Cents

By Edna Barnes

As I sat by my window watching the snow fall gently, I was reminded of Christmas. It wasn't so far away, but it seemed so to a 9-year-old. Soon I began to think about how much fun it might be to do my own shopping. In 1915 there were few opportunities to earn money, but I didn't expect to have any otherwise. Sometimes my 11-year-old sister, Mabel, and I ran errands for a neighbor who paid us a few cents, or helped our father with his chores to wheedle a penny or two from him. Pennies bought interesting trinkets.

Remembering the sign in our shoe-repair shop that read, "A Penny Saved Is a Penny Earned," I began to think that if I didn't spend every penny as soon as I received it, I might do some real shopping. It would be hard to resist temptation, but I was serious.

I cut a slit in the lid of a small box. After I'd tied a long string to it, I suspended it from the bedsprings, out of sight. Every time I received a coin, I pulled up the box, deposited it, and suspended my "bank" again.

A few days before Christmas, I showed Mabel my bank. She had a few coins, too, so we sat on the bed together and counted our savings—a grand total of 48 cents! How exciting! With so little time left, we couldn't wait to go shopping. We decided to ask Mother if we could go to town that afternoon.

We found her in the kitchen, washing clothes. Steam rose to the ceiling from a boiler on the red-hot stove, and tubs of water and clothes were everywhere. "Oh, my land, yes!" she exclaimed. "Anything to get the boys out from under my feet!"

We hadn't counted on that! "The boys" were Forrest, 6, and Manny, 4. Now we'd have our hands full. But we felt equal to it, knowing this was a special privilege for all of us.

We ran down the graveled road to the railroad tracks, the accepted route to town from our neighborhood. It was a mile to the few stores there.

A Christmas Wish by Lee H. Stroncek, courtesy of Wild Wings Inc.

Hopping and skipping along, we met two of our friends coming from town with a little white bunny. They said they had sold all of their rabbits except this one for 25 cents, and they offered it to us for 15 cents. It seemed like a bargain, but it would take a lot from our total. We sent the boys on while we pondered the decision, then finally bought it. Mabel untied the handkerchief holding our precious change. Craning my neck, I watched her remove the nickel and dime, then painstakingly tie it up again.

We whispered with the girls as to which of our brothers should have our first purchase. When this was settled, we gave them orders to take the bunny home and ask Mother to hide it in the shed.

As we ran around the bend of the tracks approaching Main Street, we caught a view of the town's colorful decorations. Our excitement mounted, and I thought the boys would burst with glee.

They ran wild when they entered the store! They seemed compelled to touch everything. The clerks must have thought the Indians had come to town celebrating, for the boys could make as much noise as a powwow.

Mabel and I planned to buy sewing baskets for each other and went straight to the notions counter. We dallied back and forth, picking up each one, inspecting it carefully for detail and price, while the clerk stood waiting. Baskets decorated with Chinese coins or jewels were more expensive so we settled for round, raffia ones with bright satin bows at 10 cents each.

Having made our most important purchases, we went to find our brothers. They had been having a good time among the toys. The clerks there were in a frenzy! Forrest was playing with a game of jacks, bouncing the ball all over the counter, while Manny was trying out a guitar! When they were asked if they had money to buy, Manny replied, "Sister's got it in 'er hankacheef."

Just then their attention was drawn to Santa, who was coming in the store with his pack of peppermint sticks. While they scurried down the aisle, we bought the guitar for a dime. Now we had something for each of us—and we had 3 cents left. We had not been concerned that we had so little, only that it must be divided as equally as possible. I wanted so much to buy something for Mother, but how could we?

We were about to leave when I saw a sign that read, "GRAB BAGS 1¢." Picking up one, I asked what was in it. The harried clerk muttered, "Hafta buy one ta find out."

This piqued our curiosity! Mabel gave her a coin and quickly untied the string on the brown paper bag. To our surprise, among some sewing needs was a pretty celluloid comb—just the thing for Mother's hair! This prompted us to buy one more. It was a greater surprise—a short pencil, on which was a holder and a small pad, just right for Papa's pocket!

With our last cent, we hugged our precious packages and bolted for the candy store. As we scrambled out the door, the clerk sighed audibly.

While we looked over the candy cases, pointing in each one with dirty fingers, all asking the price at once, the owner smiled knowingly. We were trying to get the most pieces for the penny. At last we found it! Six wrapped kisses for a cent. Mabel gave up our last coin and divided the candy: one kiss for each of us, and one for each of our parents' packages.

Merrily we skipped home. When we walked into the kitchen, Mother assured us the bunny was in safekeeping. Dashing into the living room with our bundles, we were overjoyed to see a beautiful tree! Papa had just brought it in, fresh from the woods. We placed our gifts under the tree and ran up to the attic for the shiny star and trimmings that had been carefully packed away after last Christmas.

On Christmas morning when we came downstairs, all eyes beheld the fluffy, white, pink-eared bunny, sitting on a brand-new sled under the tree, surrounded by gifts that Santa had brought. On the table sat all kinds of freshly baked Christmas goodies. We couldn't wait to show our purchases first! Mother, seeing Papa wink and smile, remarked, "You children have certainly made this a very special Christmas, proving what a small savings can do." ✷

Christmas Eve

By Janet McEwen

I t was a cold Christmas Eve in my father's dry-goods store in Bucyrus, Ohio. Stores did not display Christmas goods months ahead as they do now, but toys and gifts were put out about two weeks before the big day. Nor did stores close up at 5 or 6 o'clock on Christmas Eve, as they do now, but remained open until 10:30 or 11 p.m.

It had been a long, busy day, and now it was nearly closing time. Few customers remained and most of the clerks had already left. Business had been good that week, and shelves and cases in the toy department were noticeably depleted of their stock. Dolls had sold particularly well, but a few of the more expensive German-made ones remained.

My father noticed an old woman and little girl at the counter where some of the dolls lay in their cardboard boxes. The woman wore a shawl, the child a thin and ragged coat, small protection from the subzero weather.

He started toward them, but was called away by a clerk. As he returned, he saw the woman take one of the largest dolls and conceal it as best she could under her shawl. On seeing him, she turned her back and, taking the child by the hand, started rapidly toward the door.

He stopped her and said, "Just a minute, Lady. I saw you steal the doll. Now you know you can't do that. I'm sorry, but I will have to call the police. It's the law. You just can't do that. I'm sorry."

The old woman started to cry. "Don't do that, Mister," she pleaded. "Please don't call the law. I ain't got nothin'. An' if they lock me up, there ain't nobody to look after the girl. She ain't got no folks. I'm all she's got. I'll give back the doll, just don't send me to no jail."

She handed him the doll. By then the child was crying, too.

"All right," he said. "You can go, but don't ever come in my store again."

As they started to leave, he said, "Little girl, come back here a minute." Eyes large with fright, the youngster slowly came toward him. "Here, Honey," he said, "take the doll. It's a Christmas present from Santa Claus. Merry Christmas!"

Now, you may say that my father was wrong; that the child might think, *Even if you get caught stealing, sometimes you get a reward anyway.* But you don't know my gentle, compassionate father. Being the person he was, he could not have done otherwise.

When he told me the story years later, he said, "I thought of my three little girls at home, and of our tree loaded with their gifts from Santa and from our many relatives and friends. It was Christmas Eve, and she was just a little child." ❄

My Favorite Doll by Annable, House of White Birches nostalgia archives

Uncle Fred's Package

By Wilma Moody

I knew Christmas was on its way when my brother Jerry began asking, "Mama, did it come today?" Beginning the last week in November, Jerry would rush home from school, slam the back door and shout the same question every day until the box arrived. The rest of us children would be at his heels, anxiously awaiting Mama's answer.

I don't remember Mama ever giving a straight "Yes." She would always counter with, "You know it's too early to expect a package," or, "These are hard times. There might not be a package this year."

Such comments never fazed Jerry. He firmly believed the package would arrive. If it didn't come one day, it would be delivered the next. He was sure Uncle Fred wouldn't let us down.

Uncle Fred was a salesman for the Arm & Hammer Baking Soda Co. He drove a nice car and wore fancy clothes. We thought he was rich. He always brought us miniature sample boxes of Arm & Hammer soda, which we used to brush our teeth. Sometimes he brought candy. These small gifts were appreciated, but the arrival of his Christmas package was the highlight of the year.

Jerry had become an expert at reading Mama's face. He would say, "Now, Mama, you know it's not right to lie." Finally, the day would come when Mama had to admit the package had arrived.

From that moment until Christmas, Mama never had a minute's peace. Jerry was constantly snooping. When he could not find the Christmas box anywhere, he would insist that it was in the big locked trunk. Then we would badger Mama to just let us look at the size and feel the weight of the package. At last Mama would bring the box out of hiding and place it on the dining table so we could all get a look at it.

Next, we would plead with her to open the box and just let us see the shape of our individual gifts. But Mama's years of experience had taught her not to allow such freedom until Christmas Eve. After breakfast on that day, the gifts would be placed under the tree. By the end of the day we had thoroughly examined not only our own presents, but all the others as well.

We felt the gifts. We shook them. We smelled them. We even weighed them on the kitchen scales. We made a million guesses as to what they contained.

After supper on Christmas Eve, the long-awaited gifts were placed in our laps. When the moment finally arrived, Jerry was the last to open his present. It seemed he wanted to savor the moment for as long as possible.

Only once was I disappointed with my gift. One Christmas I received a small, green leather purse. I eagerly unfastened the clasp, expecting to find the treasures usually contained in the purses I had examined, but this new purse was only stuffed with paper to retain its shape. I threw the purse down, sobbing, and declared I did not want it.

Mama finally determined the cause of my sorrow and hurriedly placed pennies, a comb, a small mirror and a handkerchief in the purse. When she shook the purse close to my ear, I could not resist the urge to explore it. I was elated with the contents and carried the purse for many years.

Uncle Fred is gone now and so is my brother Jerry, but the joy and anticipation of Uncle Fred's packages is one of my fondest childhood memories. ✻

The Christmas Snoop

By R.G. Hobday

One of my best Christmases was almost a disaster. It was during the Great Depression— a time, I have since learned, when financial considerations often subdued dreams and wishes not only of kids, but of grown-ups, too.

We were well into the Christmas shopping season and my two brothers and I knew it was important to drop subtle hints as to what we wanted for Christmas. And of course, as Christmas approached, there was a lot of tactful—and sneaky—snooping to find out what was hidden where.

As a holdover from Santa-Claus days, the tree continued to appear after we kids had gone to sleep on Christmas Eve. It must have been difficult for the folks, but it was also economical; Christmas trees were free after 11 p.m., when the vendors abandoned them.

One year my snooping almost ruined my Christmas. I had been asking for a BB gun for years. But during my snooping, I came upon a present that could only be a guitar. Now, a guitar had been my secret wish ever since I saw my first singing-cowboy movie. I had no idea that my folks knew about it, but after all, parents were a wondrous breed apart. I could hardly wait!

Then, when Christmas finally arrived, there it was—the glorious package! But the package that was handed to me was not the guitar. When I opened it—it was the BB gun! I finally had the gift I had wanted for years—but I was still disappointed! To this day I still hope the folks didn't see how I felt.

Fortunately, I was soon having so much fun plinking at targets that I forgot all about guitars. Years later, when I finally did get one, I quickly discovered that my skills and aptitude were better suited to BB guns. ✳

Gift of Beauty

By Margaret Anthony

Christmas was celebrated twice in our family. The first celebration was for the adults on Christmas Eve. They all gathered at Grandma's house, exchanged gifts and then went to midnight mass. That was followed by breakfast at Grandma's.

Christmas Day was for the children, but when I was 12 years old I was included in the Christmas Eve celebration. I felt very grown-up. I made a special gift for Grandma to show that I was as capable of giving as receiving.

The summer of that year Grandma had taught me to knit. My knitting was slow and awkward, but my heart was in it. The Christmas gift I decided to make for Grandma was a shawl. I started working on it in November, and bought some fire-engine red yarn. Every evening, as soon as my homework was done, I worked on my knitting.

Grandma was a small woman, but she carried herself tall. Although her shoulders were somewhat stooped, no one noticed because she held her head high and walked with the grace and dignity of a queen. She dressed with great care. When she dressed for church, her simple black dress was trimmed with a snow-white collar. Her shoes were always polished, and over her shoulders she wore a white shawl.

As the enchanted hour for the exchange of gifts arrived that Christmas Eve, my heart pounded. I could hardly wait for Grandma to see the beautiful shawl I had made for her. I waited until last to give her my gift. I wanted to show it off. When Grandma unwrapped it, I heard a gasp from my Aunt Rose, but it was drowned out by Grandma's expression of surprise.

"It is beautiful," she said, and held it up. There were several places where I had dropped a stitch and a small hole appeared, and the shawl was somewhat uneven—but I didn't notice.

Soon it was time to go to midnight mass. Everyone put on their coats, and Aunt Rose brought Grandma her shawl. I looked at the shawl I'd made for Grandma, folded neatly under the Christmas tree. Grandma must have caught my look. She immediately picked it up and put it over her shoulders.

"You are not going to wear *that*," Aunt Rose said.

"Of course I am," Grandma answered. "It is my Christmas present and it is beautiful." The look in Grandma's eyes warned Aunt Rose that any further discussion was out of the question. Then Grandma took my hand and we left for church. It is a Christmas I will always remember. ❄

Fun With Yarn, House of White Birches nostalgia archives

Christmas 1932

By Molly Stewart

Had I been older, I would have known better than to ask for the doll carriage that Christmas of 1932. The strangling fingers of the Depression had already caught hold and were tightening without mercy. In our family of four girls and two boys, things were never easy. Of necessity, most of our Christmas gifts were mittens and mufflers, and socks and sweaters fashioned from old woolen garments that had been raveled, washed and reknit by our mother's creative hands.

I was the youngest of our brood, and when I was not in my first-grade classroom, I spent most of the time with my father. It was difficult enough for an able-bodied man to find a job in those days, but my father was asthmatic. I can still recall him gasping for a breath that I feared might be his last, and the self-administered injections of adrenaline that carried him through those trying times.

It was Mother, though, who first realized my desire. I was sitting at the kitchen table, painstakingly blocking out the letters to Santa, when she advanced silently to stand behind me.

"How do you spell 'carriage'?" I called loudly, not knowing anyone was near.

"C-a-r-r-i-a-g-e, dear." Her soft voice startled me and caused me to turn.

She was a striking woman, but then I guess every 6-year-old feels that way about her mother. She was tall and straight, with gentle brown eyes and thick auburn hair sprinkled with gray. Mother's dark beauty was marred only by the rough elastic bandages bound tightly around her legs to lend support while she nursed during her endless 12-hour shift at the mental hospital.

Family Circle by Lee H. Stroncek, courtesy of Wild Wings Inc.

Her hand touched my shoulder as she read the smudged letter before me. "I don't know, dear. Santa will be awfully busy this year. He has so many little boys and girls to look after. There isn't much money for him to spend, either. Many fathers are out of work. Perhaps he will have to bring food to some little people."

I didn't answer. I just sat, confidently sealing the envelope. He'd bring it. I just *knew* he'd bring the carriage. After all, I had never asked Santa for anything like this before.

Mother helped me print the address—"Santa Claus, North Pole"—and I gave the letter to her to mail.

The days passed quickly as I fingered through the slick, gaudy pages of the mail-order catalog. What would my carriage be like? It needn't be as large as the one beside the Sleeping Beauty doll. My doll, Bridget, her bald head chipped and cracked, her left leg patched with adhesive tape, would not need a big carriage like that. A small one would be fine. Santa would know.

As the big day drew nearer, the light in the kitchen burned long into the night. When Mother's working day was over and we kids were in bed, she would pull out the old treadle sewing machine and begin her next shift. I'd hear my parents' voices muffled by the whir of the machine as I snuggled deeper under the covers with visions—not of sugarplums, but of doll carriages—dancing through my head.

The day before Christmas Mother was home and, with the help of my dad and the six of us, she decorated the front room. We never had a tree, but then neither did any of our neighbors. Some faded red and green garlands were strung from the corners of the room. Where they criss-crossed in the center above the dangling light cord, we hung a silver bell. It was so beautiful, I thought, as I crouched near the potbellied heater to watch the proceedings. Would I ever be able to wait until my doll carriage arrived?

My brothers teased me as I hung my neatly mended stocking along with theirs on a line Dad had put up behind the heater. "You'll get a frozen fish in your sock, Fuzzy," they chanted. "Santa saw you snitch the cookies yesterday. You'll get a fish for sure!"

I didn't care. Let them tease. I knew Santa wouldn't forget me, even if he hadn't answered my letter. He was busy, wasn't he? All that work to do. He'd remember.

Finally Mother said it was bedtime and there was no argument that night. I closed my eyes tightly and tried hard to go to sleep. From behind the closed door I could hear their laughter and the sounds of the radio. The precious battery was usually saved for the news and the odd special program. My parents knew that once the battery was dead, the voice behind the frayed brown panel would remain silent for a long time. There was no money to be spent on luxuries.

Just when I thought sleep would never come, I must have dozed off, because when I opened my eyes, dawn was sending its reflection off the fresh snow and into my bedroom window. In the double bed across the room, my sisters still slept.

Silently I swung my feet onto the cold floor and tiptoed into the living room. My brothers were asleep on the opened Toronto couch in the corner, and I tried to be very quiet.

And then I saw it. It stood partially hidden by the heater, its blue paint bright in the early morning dusk. It was the most magnificent carriage I had ever seen. I ran toward it calling, "I knew! I knew!" caring no longer that my family slumbered.

When I reached to touch it, my joy knew no bounds. There, in the deep recess of its curved body, lay a doll more beautiful than I had ever imagined! It was dressed in high style, with a small scarf and mittens sprouting like bright red blossoms from the dark mossy green of its rough tweed coat and beret. My happiness was complete.

It wasn't until years later that I realized that neither the carriage nor the doll was new. It didn't matter then, nor does it now.

The doll's wonderful wardrobe could only have been made by my mother. I recognized the scraps of material—the cotton dirndl from the tail of Mom's faded housedress, the tweed ensemble from goods left from a skirt she had made a neighbor, the red knitted scarf and mittens. The miniature wooden suitcase covered with wallpaper had been my dad's contribution. I'll never know how they managed the doll and carriage. My sisters can't remember, and it's too late to ask Mother and Dad. But remembering that light burning long into the weary nights, how I loved them for it! ✳

Love Found a Way

By Jennie T. Beans Roberts

*I*t was during the Depression that my husband and I met and married in New England. Soon there were four small mouths to feed. I kept busy on Mother's old Singer treadle sewing machine, making the most of our clothes. One evening, without turning from my sewing, I said, "How are we ever going to make it on your part-time job?"

My husband came up behind me and kissed me on the ear. "Have faith," he said. "Everything's going to be OK." Each week thereafter, he managed to work an extra day. Even so, making ends meet was a constant struggle.

One evening a few weeks before Christmas, I told him, "We have nothing to put under the tree."

He said, "Don't worry. We'll find a way." Again he was right.

Every evening, as soon as the children were in bed, we became Mr. and Mrs. Claus. I busied myself making stocking dolls and tiny wardrobes for our two girls. My husband disappeared downstairs to the chill of the damp cellar and set to work carving toys out of scrap lumber for the two boys. Each evening we worked late into the night.

On Christmas Eve, I stood by as he painstakingly worked on the last piece of wood, the shavings falling to the floor around his feet. From his hands, red with cold, there emerged a caboose, the last car to be hooked onto the string of blue boxcars already on the counter. It was a "choo-choo" wish come true for our younger boy. At the other end of the counter, as though poised for flight, sat a wooden airplane, painted red and white. It had a 2-foot wingspan. What delight it would bring to our older son!

I marveled at this man I had married, so selflessly intent on his work. The picture of Joseph the carpenter flashed through my mind. My heart filled with joy and gratitude. *Am I feeling what Mary had felt when she watched her husband at his work?* I wondered.

Later that evening we wrapped the gifts our own hands had wrought with so much love for each other and the little ones. Then, like the Magi bearing gifts, we knelt before the tree and placed our offerings under it as lovingly as if they had been gold, frankincense and myrrh.

Our one string of lights shed a warm, rosy glow over the room. Outside, snow was falling softly. We found ourselves whispering. Then, for a few moments, we were silent. It was a holy night. Nothing before or since has brought me such joy as did giving those gifts made from love. ❄

Home for the Holidays

Chapter Three

*W*hen electricity finally made it to our little neck of the woods, the changes were immediate and profound (at least they seemed profound to us). Of course the most profound change was that of lighting the old home place. Daddy ran wires around the attic and put a single porcelain fixture in the middle of each of our three rooms.

There was no light switch; it took a lot less wiring to have a pull-chain for each light. It was magic to pull that string and flood the room with incandescence.

There were no wall outlets. That would have meant pulling walls down to run wiring, and Daddy wasn't too sure this newfound, newfangled "convenience" would be worth all that work. We were able to plug the few things that needed to be plugged into a single outlet in the light fixture. Besides lights, electricity didn't bring many changes to our lives those first couple of years.

But when Christmas rolled around that first year—now *that* was special! We always had decorated trees the old-fashioned way, with strings of popcorn, a few small ornaments and stars we three kids had cut in school and brought home to surprise Mama and Daddy.

And then there was light! It impressed me as much as if it had been the first light of Creation. And now, in the Christmas season, Daddy brought home something even more impressive—a short strand of electric Christmas lights. We sang carols as we ceremoniously draped the wires around the tree. No more would we have a drab, dark tree, lit only by the kerosene lantern. Now our front room window would gleam with the lights of the season!

But the second or third time we plugged in those lights we had a rude awakening. With an abrupt pop, the bulbs that had so brilliantly lit the tree one moment just as quickly went dark. (Many of you will remember when one burnt-out bulb meant a break in the circuit, followed by darkness.)

But Daddy had prepared for just such an "emergency" (it seemed big to us children), and had brought home a couple of extra bulbs as well. Now the only problem was the needle-in-a-haystack search for the one bulb that was the culprit. Later I wondered what we would have done if two bulbs had gone out simultaneously.

That first year, when Daddy wasn't sure that this new electrifying experience might not burn down our little home, he didn't let us leave the tree lights on all Christmas Eve. But I guess Santa must have plugged them into that porcelain light fixture, because bright and early on Christmas morning, when we piled into the still-cold, still-dark living room, the tree already glowed with the colors of the season. It was still a fairly meager yuletide, but for the first time we saw the hopeful lights of the season while we were home for the holidays back in the Good Old Days.

—Ken Tate

Trimming the Tree by Lee H. Stroncek, courtesy of Wild Wings Inc.

Home for Christmas

By Marie Wells

On that Friday afternoon in December 1923, the Christmas entertainment was over. The tree with its paper chains, silvery stars, snowflakes and other creations inspired by the children's Christmas spirit stood bare of gifts. I, the teacher in that one-room rural Nova Scotia school, viewed the thickening snowstorm with consternation; the children watched it with anticipation.

Finally, clutching their gifts, the remaining helpers sang one more chorus of *Jingle Bells*, called out, "Merry, merry Christmas!" and started home.

The last chore done, I locked the door and trudged wearily through the falling snow to my boarding place, the home of my mother's cousin. After the family supper, I helped with the dishes, put a few more things in my partially packed bag and tried to read. The hours dragged as the wind whistled and the snow whirled against the windows. At last bedtime came, and sleep finally shut out my desolation.

When Saturday morning came there was no road in sight, and some of the windows were almost covered by banks of snow, but the storm was over. It was 5 miles to the railroad station in Amherst. Could the roads be broken in time? The lump in my throat made it hard to swallow Cousin Ida's good farm breakfast. The thought of not getting home for Christmas seemed a major disaster.

The barn work done, Cousin Edgar and his son began opening a path down the long lane. Minutes seemed like hours as I watched for the road-breaking crew. Could they possibly get it opened in time for me to catch the train?

At long last came the teams of horses harnessed to bobsleds and the men with shovels. Here and there the horses could plunge through the snow as their drivers urged them on. When they came to a halt, the men went to work. Then came another advance, then another bank. At last the crew had moved out of sight—and still time dragged on!

Clapping his cold hands and stamping off the snow, Cousin Edgar finally came in. "Well, young lady, we'll try it," he said. "If the train is late, and it will be, we might make it."

It did not take me long to get into my things. Cousin Ida handed me my lunch; Greta wrapped the hot brick for the sleigh; Cousin Edgar took my bag. With a last "Merry Christmas," I tucked the buffalo robe around me and buried my mittened hands in my fur muff. Cousin Edgar shook the reins and Dinah started off, shaking her long string of bells, but rarely could she break into a trot.

My Waltham watch soon told me that it was time for my train, but we were still 3 miles away. We finally reached upper Victoria Street, where many of Amherst's well-to-do lived. Tired Dinah was urged into a trot. Soon the station came into view— and there stood the train! Would it wait until I got my ticket? I grabbed my bag, said a hurried goodbye and ran.

"All aboard!" came the call. I hesitated; the conductor beckoned. I climbed the step, was handed my bag, and collapsed into one of the few remaining seats. The day coach from Montreal was redolent with the smell of oranges, packed lunches and tired people.

The conductor gave me a ticket. The train crept forward over the icy tracks—Maccan, Nappan, Springhill Junction (a long stop for water), Salt Springs—Oxford Junction! There waited our little shortline train. Now I knew I'd get to Pugwash, but what would I do if my father could not make the 6 miles from our farm at Wallace Bay?

"Pugwash, next stop!" the conductor finally called as the train inched around a bend. The train was hours late and it was pitch-dark. I was first in line to get off the train, and the kindly conductor helped me down.

My heart sank as I walked toward the station, but at the car ahead I saw a tall shadow. There was my father! He helped me into the old raccoon coat, the extra winter wrap for returning

daughters. No one-horse sleigh awaited me, but Ned and Doll, harnessed to the bobsled. And there was still a bit of warmth in the once-hot bricks.

Again a buffalo robe was tucked in and off we started. Once out of town, our progress was slow. The road frequently wended its way through the fields to avoid snowbanks. As we came down our marsh, a few stars ventured out of the dark sky and a shadowy moon appeared. The lamplight sent a warm welcome from the kitchen window.

Soon the family was out in the wintry night to greet me, the dog wagging his tail, a brother taking my bag, Mother saying, "Come in! You must be starved!"

The black range glowed as I passed through the kitchen. A tall balsam waited in the corner of the sitting room, which, as always, was decked with boughs and streamers attached to the central hanging lamp. The old Franklin, with its wide chimney down which Santa used to slide, was ready with backlog and kindling. I quickly removed my outer wraps; tired but happy, I joined my hungry family for the belated meal.

I had made it home for Christmas. ❄

That Wonderful Time of the Year

By Mary Schaaf

As I sit in my cozy home and look out at the gentle December snow falling, I watch the landscape being transformed into an updated version of a Currier and Ives painting.

I watch the snowflakes drift slowly to the earth and my thoughts also drift back to the holiday seasons over 60 years ago in New Ulm, Minn. I loved those winter holidays more than any other holidays during the year.

On Thanksgiving, the first of the "big three holidays," all six of us rode the short distance to Uncle Alfred's house for that most unforgettable meal. That day there was newly fallen snow on the frigid ground.

Inside Ma's home place, the smell of cooking goose gave us an appetite we thought would never be satisfied. But as good as that meal was, and the pleasant conversation that followed, it was all just a warm-up for what lay ahead that evening.

After supper Daddy would tell my brothers, my sister and me to get ready and dress warmly. Then we drove uptown to see the Christmas decorations on Minnesota Street. Huge pine garlands adorned with red, blue and green lights were draped across the street, and the lights were lit for the first time on Thanksgiving night. The decorations remained the same each year, but we never tired of them. Each year it was as if we were seeing them for the first time. It was the perfect end to a perfect day. Now we were ready to get down to the business of Christmas.

The Christmas catalog had just arrived, and although being sick was never fun, it was made less painful by the fact that whoever was sick got the catalog to themselves to look at all day.

It was difficult to choose just the right toy. Ma had an uncanny knack for being able to shift our attention to toys that were within their price range. (I never realized how clever this mother of ours was until much later.) Of course, price was never a factor to us because we knew that Santa brought those toys. I could never figure out why there were prices next to the toys when they were all free.

There were no early decorations put up at our house in those days. But that didn't matter to us because we could go uptown and see enough decorations to sustain us until Christmas Eve.

My favorite window decoration was up the street at Muesing Drugstore. Animated figures were almost unheard of in those days, so I was fascinated as I watched a doll dressed in a cranberry-red gown play carols on a little pipe organ, her hands moving up and down the keyboard. The music was piped outdoors so we could stand outside that artificially snow-covered window and enjoy it.

When we finally needed to get in out of the cold, we'd head for the dime store to fulfill our reason for being uptown in the first place. We had to do our Christmas shopping!

We had saved our pennies since summer and we only had enough money to buy something inexpensive, but that never mattered to Ma or Daddy. I guess it gave meaning to the saying, "It's the thought that counts."

Daddy's gift was never a problem. It was the same each year. We'd bound into Hans Schnieder's tobacco store and order several White Owl cigars.

Ma's gift took a lot more thought. We'd wander up and down the aisles of the dime store, looking for just the right gift. Invariably we'd end up with hankies. We were proud of our purchases and made our way home to wrap and hide our treasures.

While we were in town, we'd walk up and down the toy aisles of Retzlaff Hardware Store and make a mental note of what we'd ask Santa for when he visited our town in early December.

We would anxiously await this visit of St. Nick. To keep us in tow, Ma would threaten us by saying that if we didn't behave, St. Nick would pass by our house. But without fail, on the morning of Dec. 6, we found four little bags sitting in the shanty, each filled with an apple or orange and some peanuts. We never did receive the dreaded piece of coal.

Now it was time for Ma to bake her delicious Christmas cookies. There were several kinds, but the best by far were her sugar cookies. Some were frosted and some had only colored sugar on them, but all were cut into shapes of Christmas trees, stars, lions and a few gingerbread men. These were carefully placed in dishpans, canners and whatever big kettle was available, then stored in the cellar.

Then Ma would shop for the Christmas candy—haystacks, chocolate stars, cremes, hard and filled candies, along with an assortment of nuts. All the bags were also hidden down in the cellar.

It didn't take us long to uncover the cache, however, and whenever Ma went somewhere, we'd stage a raid. We were smart enough not to take too much. I'm sure Ma knew what was going on, but she never mentioned it.

Christmastime at our parochial school was also full of anticipation. We practiced hymns and carols. The nuns had their own way of keeping our hyperactivity to a minimum. From time to time, Santa paid a visit to school, roaming the halls and ringing a bell. None of us ever saw him, and I suspect that it was one of the nuns sneaking up and down the halls. But whoever it was, the idea worked.

The Friday before vacation we had our big Christmas party. Then we finally got to see that elusive Santa. He'd bound into the hall with a large sack on his back. Leo Schuck was the most authentic Santa I have ever seen. For years, this wonderful man took time off work to bring joy to kids in New Ulm. I don't know if he ever received recognition, but he certainly deserved a medal.

We also staged a short program, which usually included a skit. One of these programs almost resulted in tragedy. My brother, Benny, was playing the part of Scrooge. He was seated next to a fireplace, which had a big clock atop the mantel. As the curtain rose, it caught the cover on the fireplace and the clock came crashing down on Scrooge's head. Thankfully, Benny didn't become the ghost of Christmas Past; only his pride was hurt.

After we all had received our bag of candy from Santa, we were dismissed for the holidays.

Now we were Ma's problem.

Finally Christmas Eve arrived. Once again, Daddy would pack his little family into the car and take us to Uncle Alfred's home. Much to our surprise, Santa had been there and left gifts for all of us.

We were so engrossed in our gifts that we never noticed that Daddy had left. Not until years later did we figure out that he had hurried home to help Ma decorate our tree and the house and put our presents under the tree. But we never questioned this ritual. It was all part of the tradition.

All too soon, Ma and Daddy both returned to take their brood home. There was still one more tradition to observe, however. Every year, Benny had to sing *Oh, Tannenbaum*—much to his dismay. The rest of us snickered because we knew how much he hated to sing in front of everyone.

When we got home we were very surprised to see that while we were gone, Santa had paid a visit to our house, too. We *ooed* and *aahed* at our beautiful tree. It bore only a single string of eight lights, but in our children's eyes, they looked like hundreds.

The boughs were laden with dozens of colorful old German ornaments of every size and shape. There were also six decorated anise cookies hanging on the tree. Ma bought these cookies each year.

After we had spent enough time savoring the aroma of the tree and its decorations, it was time to see if Santa had brought what we had requested. Our gifts from Santa were never wrapped. They were right there, in plain sight, ready to be wound up, sat on, played upon or experimented with.

Ah, but there was more! Those beautifully wrapped packages that had arrived from Aunts Frances, Barbara and Katie still had to be opened. Aunt Barbara and Aunt Frances always sent beautiful and practical gifts such as dresses, slips, mittens and shirts.

The most sought-after gifts, however were the ones from Aunt Katie. That lady knew what kids like for Christmas—things totally useless and impractical for a kid growing up in the Depression. Ma couldn't figure out why Aunt Katie would send such worthless things as big, fuzzy, white mittens, purses and comb-and-brush sets. I can't remember what the boys received, but I'm sure it was something equally useless in the eyes of a responsible adult.

After all the gifts were opened, we had to carefully fold the wrapping paper. It was saved and would be ironed later, to be used again the following year. Nothing was wasted.

After the hustle and bustle settled down, we were herded off to bed. Tomorrow, Christmas Day, would begin with Mass and a time to reflect on the true meaning of this wonderful time of year.

It was hard to wake up and twice as hard to leave behind our new treasures as we sat through High Mass, but the sight that greeted us as we entered church was worth any inconvenience.

The Christmas crib was nestled among freshly cut balsams. The aroma spread throughout the church. Trees on each side of the altar were hung with lights of every color. After Mass we all marched up to the crib single-file to see the Baby Jesus in the manger. A small offering box sat alongside the crib, and each of us put our pennies into the box.

Soon we were back home, to continue where we had left off. That day, and every Christmas, was spent with just the six of us. We enjoyed a wonderful chicken dinner, and it was a relaxing relief after all the rushing around of the previous few weeks. I can still see Daddy sitting and smiling as he watched us play with those toys that he and Ma had so carefully chosen.

The sounds of happy children filled the house. The constant tooting of my sister's Teddy Tooter pierced the quiet, as did the toy train that whistled as it rounded the tracks. The smell from the chemistry set was enough to spoil one's appetite, but it wasn't bad enough to keep me from plunking away on my new toy piano.

Was it any wonder that Daddy's hair was snow-white and Ma's nerves were a mess?

As kids do the world over, we did eventually tire of playing with our new toys. Ma took advantage of this short-lived respite; it was the perfect time to get us to write our thank-you notes. None of us enjoyed the task as we pondered over what to say to someone who was twice our age. It took the better part of the day, and that was just what Ma had been hoping for. The peace and quiet were very much appreciated. And although we dreaded this part of the holiday ritual, it taught us valuable lessons that we carried with us throughout our lives. Respect, thankfulness and responsibility never go out of style.

As soon as weather permitted, we went outside to see if that new sled performed as advertised. We really enjoyed the outdoors. We had a nice hill to ski and sled on right outside our door. And Ma could keep an eye on us. She was thrilled to see us wear ourselves out on that hill. We were wet when we came in, but this was one time Ma didn't mind, for we were also very tired. I'm sure this is what a mother's dreams are made of.

All too soon our vacation came to an end. But our beautiful tree would remain up until at least Jan. 6, or longer if it wasn't dropping too many needles. It was a sad day when it finally came down.

Now all the gifts that had remained under the tree to be shown off to company were finally put away. A few nuts remained, and a few Christmas cookies still had to be eaten, but by and large, Christmas was over for another year.

I have gathered a few toys that have survived the years, and I place them under our tree every year. My doll buggy is missing a few hubcaps and the celluloid windows are broken. My doll's face and legs are cracked from age. My little wooden ironing board looks the best; the years have been good to it. I can still read its price— 49 cents—on its bottom.

As I sit and look at those presents, I remember how happy they and so many others, now long gone, made one freckle-faced, pigtailed little girl way back then. Whatever happened to the chemistry set, train, gas station, sled and other toys? Who could have known that if we had all those toys today, they would fetch a nice price at an antique show?

I still have a few ornaments that hung on our tree in the 1920s, 1930s and 1940s. They occupy a prominent place on my tree now.

If I could have one wish for Christmas, it would be that every child could be as happy as we were in those Good Old Days, when Santa brought us simple but wonderful presents. I know that I never said it often enough then, but to Ma and Daddy, I say, "Thank you!" They helped make Christmas a truly wonderful time of year. ✳

PERSIS CLAYTON WEIRS
1999 ©

Our Christmas Traditions

By Benita Davidson

I grew up during the Great
Depression of the 1930s. Even
then, Christmas was a special time
of the year for our family, but there's
one yuletide that stands out above all the others
in my memory.

We were living at Beaumont Mill Village,
near Spartanburg, S.C., in the upper Piedmont,
where my Daddy was a textile worker. But the
mill was curtailing; he only worked two or three
days every other week. It was hard to feed and
clothe a family of seven on that, so Mama made
most of our clothing and household linens. She
also sewed for other people to supplement our
income. Fortunately, we never went cold, hungry
or ragged, as many poor children did then.

The holiday season was upon us before
we knew it, but the prospects of a prosperous
Christmas celebration looked slim. We had no
money for extras, like presents.

Then Mama came up with a great idea.
"We're going to have an old-fashioned Christmas this year," she announced, "just like we
had when I was a child!" We were so excited.
Our favorite pastime was listening to her stories
about growing up "back home" in the mountains of North Carolina.

The air was crisp, but we bundled up warmly.
Loading the younger children onto my brother's
red wagon, we headed for the nearby woods.
There we found our Christmas tree, a shapely
pine. We gathered cedar branches, too, and lots
of holly with bright red berries.

Back home, Mama brought out a single string
of lights (our first) and some shiny ornaments
leftover from better times. We made more decorations. When we had decorated it, we thought it
was the most beautiful Christmas tree in the
whole world!

Mama decorated the house with fragrant
boughs of cedar and holly, hanging it over the
mirrors and pictures, laying a spray on each
mantelpiece, and making a huge wreath tied
with a big red bow for the front door.

That afternoon she baked a fresh coconut
cake, a chocolate cake and pumpkin pies. We
cut out gingerbread boys and decorated them

with raisins. The best part was eating the broken
cookies afterward.

The next day, a U.S. Mail truck stopped in
front of our house! It brought a box of red apples
and a sack of black walnuts from Mama's uncle
in North Carolina.

Granny came early on Christmas Eve, bringing good things to eat from the farm. Mama
roasted a big hen and fixed all the trimmings.
She covered the table with a red checked cloth
and set out her best dishes and silverware.

When Daddy came home from work, the
house was filled with a delicious aroma. He
carried a huge sack of oranges over his shoulder
and held a big box of stick candy under his arm.
At 6 p.m., he brought in the yule log and laid it
on the fire with great ceremony. "Christmas will
last until every bit of this log has burned to ashes,"
he told us. We hoped it would never go out.

I recall vividly the beauty of that night as we
walked home from church with gifts under our
arms. Then a soft snow began to fall.

We gathered around the fireplace. Mama lit
the old kerosene lamp that she and Daddy had
started keeping house with, and set it on the
mantelpiece. She read us the story of Christ's
birth from the second chapter of Luke. Then we
sang Christmas carols for Daddy, hung our
stockings by the fireplace and went to bed.

We were up before daybreak to see if Santa
had visited us. Our stockings bulged with
goodies. Beneath the tree we found beautifully
dressed dolls in tiny beds, a handsome game
table with a checkerboard painted right on it, a
set of checkers and a tiny set of dishes. There
was even a new dress for each of us girls.
Mine was red velvet!

The house was cold, so Daddy got up and
chased us back to bed until he could roust the
fire, but we took our stockings with us and
feasted on the goodies. It's a wonder we weren't
sick from eating fruit, candy and nuts on empty
stomachs, but we were too happy to be sick.

Looking back, I realize that it took a lot of
work for our parents to give us a big Christmas
that year, but I'm sure it was a labor of love.
Daddy had built the game table and doll beds on

nights leading up to Christmas long after we slept. Mama had sewed far into the night, fixing up our old dolls and making new dresses for us from hand-me-downs.

Many a Christmas has come and gone since then; some of them were happy, and some sad. We children grew up, married and were scattered to the four winds, in Louisiana, Georgia, Kentucky, Virginia, Washington, D.C., Michigan, Montana and even Japan. We buried Granny in 1945, and Daddy and one grandchild in 1955.

When we were grown and no longer together, our greatest happiness was receiving a card, a letter or a package from our loved ones so far away. Best of all was a phone call; how wonderful just to hear their voices!

In our own homes, we kept some of the traditions that our family had started on that long-ago Christmas.

In 1980, the hand of fate brought each of us back to South Carolina, searching for our family roots. That year we had an old-fashioned Christmas, just like the ones we had as children! We made gifts for each other, and ornaments for the tree. We made gingerbread boys, too, and let the children help. We lit the same old kerosene lamp and read the Christmas story from the family Bible. Then we sang carols and watched the yule log glow.

But most of all, we remembered that never-to-be-forgotten Christmas, when we were so poor money-wise, but still wealthy beyond all comparison! ❊

When Christmas Came to Our House

By Beatrice Drummond

When Christmas came to our house
In days of long ago,
We didn't have big snowplows
To scrape away the snow.
The lanes were sometimes drifted o'er
As we all traveled home;
My mom and dad would anxious grow
And hoped we all could come.

We didn't have a store-bought tree
Of silver, pink or gold;
We had the good old-fashioned kind
We chopped, out in the cold!
We'd place it on the big farm sled
Behind the horses gray,
As through the woods we'd head for home
With hearts so light and gay.

On Christmas Eve we'd trim the tree;
It was a pleasant chore.
We'd stand back and admire our work
A dozen times or more!
We didn't have electric lights
Like modern folks do now.
We trimmed the tree in our own way,
For Mother showed us how.

Our strings of popcorn added much
To make our tree look gay,
And ropes of berries made it bright
In candle's flickering play.
We'd add a pinecone here and there
Upon the branches, too,
And little things we each had made
As we as children do.

Some candy canes were hung upon
The branches firm and green.
A big bright star was placed on top
Where it could well be seen!
When all the trimming had been done,
We'd sit a spell and rest,
With cocoa and some homemade fudge—
Mom's always was the best!

On Christmas Day we shared our gifts;
We did as we could afford,
For after all, Christmas is
To honor our dear Lord!
And so as memories come and go,
They sometimes bring a tear,
For when Christmas came to our house,
It was a special day, each year!

For Unto Us A Child Is Given

By Verla Mooth

All through the pre-Christmas days of 1952, our precious 3-year-old son, Dirk, had been asking Santa Claus to bring him a pair of cowboy boots, a gun and holster, a "pickatar" (a guitar) and a baby sister. The desire for a baby sister had been planted in his little mind in September, when he was moved into a twin bed in an effort to prepare him for sharing his life with a new baby.

We expected an addition to our family because the Chicago Foundlings Home, from which we had adopted Dirk as a baby, had informed us that they would have a baby girl for us by Christmas. Our hearts were filled with joy at the prospect of a second child. We were so fortunate to even be considered for another baby. So many other couples couldn't even get one!

I had redecorated the children's bedroom, making it suitable for both a boy and girl. Dirk's side of the room had a Western motif, and on the wall above the baby's bed, little rabbits played in clumps of green grass. Both the rabbits and cowboys had been cut from printed chintz and pasted on the newly painted walls.

Everything was ready, but something seemed to be holding things back. Then I learned that some of the medical tests I had taken turned out poorly, and I was asked to take them over.

Dec. 22 arrived and we were still waiting. The cowboy boots, gun and holster, "pickatar" and other toys were gaily wrapped and hidden away for Santa Claus to deliver. But what would we tell our disappointed little boy if his baby sister did not arrive by Christmas Day? The question filled our minds with anxiety. I started praying in earnest.

On top of all this, the winter of 1952 was promising to be a severe one. Snow had been falling for most of December and the streets of Chicago were rutted and filled with ice. Even with tire chains, it was almost impossible to travel the streets. The snow was making life much more difficult!

And then my prayers were answered. The Chicago Foundlings Home called and said we could come and see our little girl that day, but we could not take her home until the 24th—Christmas Eve. We were bursting with excitement as we took Dirk down to see our new baby.

She was a precious little girl with fat, chubby cheeks. The nurses lovingly called her Bonnie Butterball, but we had chosen the name

Paula. After holding her in my arms, it was difficult to relinquish her for two more days.

When the morning of Christmas Eve arrived, everything was prepared to go get our little girl. A bag of baby clothes and a soft, pink blanket were placed in our car.

When we arrived at the home, there was much excitement. Three babies had been placed in baby seats under the lighted Christmas tree in the old-fashioned parlor. *Chicago News* photographers were taking pictures of the Christmas babies that were to go to their new homes. The pictures were to be featured on the front page on Christmas Day. I thought with pride that our little girl was the most beautiful of the three. I am sure the other parents felt the same.

My mother, who was housemother at the Foundlings Home, was coming home with us to spend the Christmas holidays. We thought it best for her to sit in the back and hold the baby so Dirk would not feel pushed aside. It was a slow and difficult trip home, but we finally arrived safely.

My husband's parents were invited for Christmas dinner and to see our new baby. I had lots of work yet to do, but the baby was very fussy in her new home. It was not a good Christmas Eve! I was up all night, and looking out the window, I discovered that it had started to snow again. By morning, the streets were completely covered. Not one car ventured out. By midmorning, 18 inches of new snow had fallen.

Dirk woke at the crack of dawn and rushed eagerly in to the tree to see what Santa had left him. He was not disappointed. The sound of tearing paper soon revealed that all his requests had been granted. And there was no doubt about his baby sister being there. Her cries filled the room!

After breakfast, I busied myself with feeding and bathing the baby while my mother put the turkey in the oven. By midmorning the entire house was filled with enticing aromas.

And then the phone rang! It was my mother-in-law, and she was crying; my father-in-law refused to venture out in the snowstorm. She wouldn't get to have Christmas with us or see the baby. To my deep consternation, my husband assured her that he would come after her.

It took two hours to shovel out our driveway and three hours to make the 10-mile round trip. He lost count of the times he got stuck in the snow. Christmas dinner was much later than planned, but we finally sat down together and gave thanks to God for all His blessings.

The snow finally stopped at about noon and the snowplows started clearing the streets. Before dark, my father-in-law decided he would come after my mother-in-law and have some of the leftovers. I was truly happy that my husband would not have to go out again.

By dark, one very tired little boy was ready for bed. He wanted to sleep with his gun and holster and pickatar. His boots were placed beside his bed.

We whispered our prayers, for his baby sister was already asleep. It was the beginning of a lifetime of loving and sharing.

After my mother and my husband had gone to bed, I took advantage of the first quiet moments that I had to be alone all day. I went into the living room where the glowing embers in the fireplace and the lights of the tree reflected their shining pattern through the window onto the snow. It was so beautiful!

I felt a deep peace in my heart and my eyes filled with tears of unspeakable gratitude to God for His wonderful gift. I knew that the tiny baby girl who had become ours this Christmas would change our world forever. I also thanked Him for the gift of the Christ Child who came to earth so long ago and likewise changed the world forever.

As the last embers of the fire died, I turned off the tree lights and prepared for bed. In the distance I heard the chimes of church bells. Or was it the angels singing, "Glory to God in the highest and peace on earth to men of good will"?

In every fiber of my being, I joined in the sweet refrain, "For unto us a Child is given. Alleluia! Alleluia!"

Christmas 1952 remains a living memory. That holiday brought us a gift that grows more priceless with the passing years—a tiny baby girl named Paula. ✳

Christmas Trimmings by Charles Berger, House of White Birches nostalgia archives

Christmas on the Farm

By Louise Mattax

Our first Christmas on the farm would have been a scanty one without my parents' imagination and cleverness, and without my grandparents and aunts. Mama always raised a few turkeys. They ran loose in the pasture and woods where they could pick up bugs, seeds and acorns. Then, in the fall, we made a little outing out of hunting for the turkeys. We really didn't go far, but to us girls it seemed a long distance, for we went out of sight of the farm buildings.

The woods were quiet and dark and we could imagine all sorts of things, especially with Daddy's help! When he found toadstools, spied tiny footprints and heard small voices, what a delicious chill ran up our spines!

Once we caught the turkeys, we tied their legs and placed them on a cart to pull them home. Mama sold all but a couple in town and used the money for Christmas and to buy material for school dresses. But one special turkey was penned up to fatten for our Christmas dinner.

At Christmas, we cut a cedar in the woods and trimmed it with old Christmas cards and popcorn strings—the usual thing in those days.

Daddy got some orange crates and used them to make us a gorgeous set of table and chairs painted black and trimmed in red. He built them in the barn, a place out-of-bounds to us, so he was safe from our prying eyes. We enjoyed those little chairs and that table for many years.

Mama cut cardboard into shapes, then covered them with waste cotton from the fields and glued on bits of calico with flour paste to make furniture for our dolls. And what pretty furniture it was! Of course, our dolls got new dresses, too.

Early on Christmas morning, we heard noises on the roof. Daddy and Mama said they thought Santa Claus was just leaving. Before we could get our shoes and coats, we heard the sleigh bells. But when we looked outside, there, coming up the path, were two aunts with cookies and candy from Grandma and Grandpa. Years later, we learned that the aunts had tossed pebbles onto the roof and had rung a handbell.

Our childish innocence made this a wonderful Christmas. We really thought we could see Santa Claus among the trees!

Mama was a good cook. From her French background she had learned to make *polenta*, a kind of mush with meat broth and shreds of meat. From Daddy's mother she learned to make a black-eyed sop, ham liquor with hot black coffee added to it, which was really good over biscuits.

She also baked cakes, cured sausages and did all kinds of wonderful things with vegetables. And her pies—Daddy always said he only liked three kinds of Mama's pies: closed, open-faced and crisscross! One year when we had a fruit failure, Mama made a green tomato pie and it was good, too. She often made squash pies instead of pumpkin, and we liked them best of all.

So Christmas dinner consisted of vegetables that had been kept in the cellar, pies from dried peaches and apples and, of course, the turkey.

Daddy raised peanuts. Mama roasted some in the oven and we used them to make Christmas brittle.

Did you ever have snow ice cream? That year we had a nice snow and Mama brought in a pail of it. She mixed Guernsey cream with sugar, flavoring and eggs, then carefully folded it into the snow. This was heaven to us! We enjoyed it that afternoon after the dishes were done, presents were opened, and our toys enjoyed, and before Grandma, Grandpa, Aunt Evaline and Stella left.

We had many Christmases when times were better, but that first Christmas is the one I remember best.

I suppose by today's standards we were poor, but we felt rich! ❄

Special Delivery: Original Art by Tom Browning

Christmas on the Prairie

By Cherise Wyneken

It was Christmastime—a time when memories mingle with the scents of candles, pine, cinnamon, molasses, brown sugar and chocolate birthday cake. "Found you on the doorstep," Daddy always said, "one snowy Christmas Eve."

Shelly was too much like him to believe it. Mama's stories—how the doctor ate her Christmas goodies and played with Wade's new train while waiting for the birth—were enough proof for Shelly.

People always asked her if she felt short-changed. But she never did. Her Christmas birthday always seemed quite special.

Once, she begged to have a party. Mama stalled, "Next year." Seeing Shelly's disappointment, she added, "You can let your cousin Margaret spend the night if you wish."

Shelly's upstairs room was like an attic, open to the rafters. Wind whistled through the shingles as the girls snuggled under Gramma's wool-stuffed quilts.

"Aren't you excited?" Margaret kept saying. "You get to have a party next year!"

Next year is far away, Shelly mused. *Why get excited now?*

But Margaret knew that Mama already had made invitations and asked Teacher to distribute them to all the girls in class. The very next afternoon, Shelly's teacher and her classmates began appearing at the door. Shelly was confused until she saw that Mama had everything arranged—games like hunt-the-peanuts, prizes, gifts, birthday cake and ice cream.

Now it was Christmas again.

"Hurry with your dusting," Mama said. "Gramma and Grampa will be here soon. Then it will be time for Santa."

A light snow was falling, hiding the last rays of sunlight. Darkness melted into corners of the cozy house. The two matching living- and dining-room linoleum rugs that Mama was so proud of shone with new wax. The windows sparkled clear and clean. The potbellied stove in a corner of the dining room gave a friendly roar as Daddy opened it to add more coal. In the living room, beside the western window, stood the Christmas tree.

Here and there on full green boughs hung bright, fragile ornaments in the shapes of teapots, birds, bells and balls. Tinsel icicles sparkled when Mama brushed against them. She was attaching the last candle to the end of a branch, making sure it didn't touch the needles. Since it was dangerous to have live candles on a tree, they would be lighted only once—tonight—Christmas Eve.

"Oh no!" Shelly cried. "I spilled some polish on the floor."

"Don't worry." Mama wiped it with a cloth. "See? It helps to make it shine. There, I guess we're ready now. Hurry and get cleaned up. Put your new dress on so Santa Claus can see it, too."

They had chosen it from pictures in the *Sears & Roebuck* catalog. Deep red, the color of port wine, it had tiny ecru flowers and a lace collar. The sleeves were long and full. Surely it would be the prettiest dress at the children's program later at church. Shelly could hardly contain herself, thinking of all the exciting things to come.

"Merry Christmas! Merry Christmas!" called Gramma, Grampa and Uncle Elmer as they came in through the kitchen door. They stomped the snow off their galoshes onto Mama's braided rug. Grampa and Uncle Elmer carried bushel baskets of wrapped packages and spread them on the floor below the tree.

"Happy birthday, little girl," Uncle Elmer said, picking Shelly up and twirling her around.

The family gathered around the table in the dining room for the birthday dinner. After cake and candles, Mama and Gramma cleared away the dishes and cleaned up.

Wade went to the window by the tree. "Let's watch for Santa."

By now it had turned pitch-dark. The light from inside spread across the hard, white snow. Wade and Shelly stared at the open fields. But once again they missed Santa's arrival, for they didn't hear him until he came clumping down the stairs.

"Ho, ho, ho! Merry Christmas! Merry Christmas!" There he stood, red and round, his fluffy, white beard bouncing with each word.

Shelly was terrified. Her stomach turned to stone and tingles danced inside her head. She didn't hear a word he said as she watched him talk to Wade. Then he turned to her.

"And now little girl, what is *your* name? How old are you? What grade are you in school?"

Shelly answered each question in a weak and wobbly voice. Then came the dreaded inquiry: "Have you been a good girl?"

"I—I—I think so."

"Well then, if you can say your Christmas piece for me, I'll see if old Santa's bag has something nice for you."

Shelly was sure it would not be *half* so hard to say her piece at the program later at church. *Ordinary* people would be sitting in the pews.

When Santa left, they gathered by the tree. Mama lit the candles and turned out the other lights. Shelly didn't notice Uncle Elmer sneak back in. She was entranced by the yellow flames that danced and flickered, and the fragrant smell of melted wax that enveloped the warm room. It seemed to Shelly that no palace could compare. She and Wade held hands before the Christmas tree and sang *Away in a Manger*. Then everyone joined with *Silent Night*.

At last the gifts were distributed and Mama said, "We'd better blow the candles out." Mama was afraid of fire. They turned the lights back on and opened their gifts.

Santa never failed. Each got that special thing he or she wanted. The children knew their parents didn't have much money. They seemed to sense their limits. Shelly got more gifts then the others; no one had forgotten that it was also her birthday.

Now they had to hurry. The church program would be starting soon. There would be plenty of time tomorrow to play with their new toys. Snow lay deep upon the roads. Grampa harnessed his old horse and took them in the sleigh.

When they got to the church, the children found the places that had been reserved for them in the front rows. How different it felt from the rehearsals! Now the ceiling lights were casting a dull gleam over the filling pews. Up front stood a tall tree, its star-tipped top almost touching the ceiling. Bright electric bulbs in all the colors of the rainbow glittered from its branches. When the other lights went out, the church turned into a fairyland. Shelly caught her breath, enchanted.

After all the recitations were said, all the prayers were prayed, and all the songs were sung, the lights came on again. Shelly blinked against the brightness. One of the men stepped forward and asked the people to be seated.

Daddy and three other men brought boxes up the aisle and began distributing bags of candy to the children—candy canes and peanuts, hard red-and-green log candies with colored flower centers, and others that looked like giant Zs. Every child got one. Shelly felt proud to see Daddy helping.

As soon as they were finished, Aunt Dorothy played the postlude on the old pump organ. People greeted one another before they turned to leave.

Most went directly home, but not Shelly's family. For them, Christmas was not over. They said goodnight to Gramma and Grampa with the promise of dinner on Christmas Day. Then they walked toward town to their other Gramma's apartment in the old hotel. Her other children were gathered there from out of town. All her spare rooms were filled that night. Santa had been there, too, and left everyone a gift.

Heaping plates of round, white cookies sprinkled with red candies and frosted ginger cookies were waiting for them. After the cookies and hot cocoa, Shelly began to nod. Didn't grown-ups ever tire? At last they grouped around the black upright piano with its yellowed keys and sang along as Daddy's older brother, Shorty, played the chords.

"Goodbye! Goodbye! God bless you! Merry Christmas! Happy New Year!" It seemed to take forever to tell each one farewell.

The four of them buttoned their coats and drew scarves around their mouths for the walk home through the silent night. The air was crisp and cold. The stars were diamonds in the sky. The only sound was the crunch of their footsteps on the newly fallen snow.

Sometime that night it began to snow again. But Wade and Shelly slept peacefully in their attic rooms, unmindful of the soft flakes drifting through the wooden beams onto their warm, woolen quilts. ❊

An Old-Fashioned Christmas

By Mrs. H. Whipple

Give me an old-fashioned Christmas
With the ground all covered with snow;
When all those who roam shall try to get home,
No matter how far they must go.
Give me a bright, cozy kitchen
With everyone busy and gay;
Where it smells so nice with foods that entice,
Each a favorite for Christmas Day.
Give me the family all together,
Each one in their usual place,
Where the feasting is done with such cheer and fun
And a smile upon each face.

Give me a Christmas where folks drop in,
Where there are moments to reminisce;
Where there are children about to laugh and shout
And plenty of holiday bliss.
Give me a tree from the forest
That is fresh and fragrant and green;
One trimmed with delight till it's festive and bright
And really quite splendid to see …
Where family tradition is followed
And loved as the holiday nears …
Every trinket and ball is cherished by all
And treasured throughout the years.

Give me a Christmas with gifts of love
Though they might be simple and small;
When folks really care and kind thoughts are there,
I surely shall treasure them all.
Give me a Christmas where love abounds
And Christ is the honored guest,
Where the church bells ring and people all sing
And the day is specially blessed.

Give me a Christmas so pleasant
That it shall remain in my heart,
And in each future year when memories appear,
It shall be a Christmas apart.

Christmas 1912

By Kathryn W. Smith

Our first house, built by Mother, Dad, Sister and I, was complete. It was a brown-shingled, three-bedroom house with a cobblestone foundation and fireplace. My sister and I had gathered those stones all over the neighborhood and carried them home in a small wagon. Building our home was truly a labor of love.

Now we were making plans for our first holiday in our new home. Mother had a real talent for teaching us many different activities. She liked to plan parties, family events and learning experiences. In preparation for Christmas, she made different kinds of candy—chocolate fudge, penuche, divinity and marshmallows—both to be given as gifts and to enjoy ourselves. The marshmallows took a long time. They were made with gelatin and had to be beaten in a large kettle for a long time using a dough hook. When the mixture could be handled, it was turned out into a pan and left to harden. Then the marshmallows were cut into squares.

Taffy-pulling was the theme of one pre-Christmas party. It was a sticky mess, but fun. The syrup was cooked until, when tested in a cup of cold water, the syrup snapped. The mixture was poured into a pan and left until it was cool enough to handle, then two people pulled it. We covered our hands with butter to keep the candy from sticking, then pulled it back and forth, folded it over and pulled it again, until it was too stiff to pull any more. Then we broke the candy into small pieces.

We made popcorn balls, too, shaping the syrup-coated popcorn with our buttered hands. Once we had added loops of string, these were ready to hang on the Christmas tree. We strung cranberries and popcorn to hang on the tree as well, and made daisy chains from colored craft paper. We didn't have tinsel or colored lights. Our tree was lit by small candles in holders that snapped onto the branches. It was a beautiful sight.

We made ornaments out of old greeting cards, valentines and bits of yarn made into small dolls. We had very few tree ornaments that were not homemade.

We kept a barrel of McIntosh apples in the cellar where it was so cold that they didn't spoil through the winter months. We were welcome to help ourselves from the barrel whenever we wanted. The apples had other uses, too. We helped Mother make mincemeat for the holidays. She used beef in her mincemeat, and apples, of course, plus raisins, citron and other fruit and spices. She might have added some brandy, too. When the mincemeat was finished, she packed it in a large crock and put it in the cellar beside the apple barrel. Whenever Mother sent one of us to get some mincemeat for a pie, we always managed to eat an extra spoonful on the spot. As it aged, I remember nothing that tasted quite so good.

Our Christmas presents were usually things we made for each other. Each year, Mother made new wardrobes for our dolls, old or new. One year we wanted baby dolls, and another year brides, and Mother always made the appropriate clothes. For the brides, she made complete trousseaus and the most beautiful wedding gowns. She filled small trunks with these lovely things. Our great-aunt, who spent time with us while she was going to business school, liked to crochet and knit, and she made us warm slippers each year, and sometimes new scarves and caps.

In 1912, even Dad went on a sewing streak. He made us reversible coats, plaid on one side and dark blue on the other, with silk braid binding. He also made a bathrobe for Mother. He had never done this before, but I remember that the results were lovely, and the garments he made lasted for a good number of years.

We looked forward to the day when the large boxes arrived from Washington state, from our grandparents and Aunt Effie and Uncle Joe. Mother was like a child when these boxes arrived. She could open them without unwrapping them by tearing a small hole in one corner

Getting Ready for Christmas by Jay Killian, House of White Birches nostalgia archives

and reaching in and feeling around. Then she knew exactly what was in each box.

Grandma's always had holly on top, with red and orange berries. It grew in her front yard in Bellingham, Wash. We had never seen holly growing and always enjoyed receiving the sprigs she put in our Christmas package.

Aunt Effie and Grandma knitted things for us, and also embroidered nightgowns and lovely doilies for Mother, some of which I still have.

We hung our stockings on our fireplace. We knew what we would find in the morning, but it was always fun to go through the pretense of not knowing. There was always an orange in the toe

of each stocking, a few walnuts and other nuts, and an apple. That was it.

We didn't have money for extravagant gifts and we were happy with what we had. Each year we were asked what we wanted more than anything, and that was what we received. It was usually a new doll. I always wanted a dark-haired one and always seemed to get a blonde. I still have the last one I received, a blond baby doll, now over 80 years old.

I can't remember a happier Christmas than the one in 1912. It was simple, but filled with love and the pleasures of happy family life. What more could one ask? ❋

Trees & Cherished Traditions

Chapter Four

Even though we were raised out on the farm, each Christmas Eve we would bundle up for a drive to the nearest town, about 10 miles away. There we did our last-minute shopping, and afterwards we walked and drove around the city, looking at Christmas lights.

Christmas lights were a novelty to a lot of folks. Those were hard times. Some people didn't even have electricity, and many of the lucky ones who had electricity couldn't afford elaborate Christmas displays.

Still, most of the storefronts carried the signs of the season. There were rows of brightly colored lights, manger scenes, decorated trees, holly wreaths—all in displays framed by picture windows that were just perfect for a little boy on tiptoes to strain for a look.

My older brother, Dennis, and I would rush down the bustling walk-ways from store to store, excitedly chattering about all of the sights our young eyes were drinking in. Carolers here and there spiced the frosty air with, "God rest ye, merry gentlemen …" A Salvation Army group trumpeted the season while looking for a few pennies or nickels to help the needy.

Looking in a toy-store window and knowing Daddy was nearby, we always ran through an old ritual. First Dennis intoned, "Wow! Looky at the (insert whatever toy we might want for gift)!"

Then I chimed in, "Daddy, do you think Santy Claus could bring us one of those?"

Daddy responded, "I don't know. It's been a tough year and Santa has a lot of little boys who would like one."

"Well, what do you s'pose he'll bring us?"

"Oh, a bundle of switches or a lump of coal …" Daddy laughed to let us know it was just a joke.

All around us, other families participated in their own family Christmas rituals of love. And there, on a busy city street, I came to understand a basic truth of life: The spirit of the season simply overpowered the problems of the day. The love of individual families spilled across social and cultural boundaries and—just for a little while—all the love of those families covered the sidewalks and street just like December's snows.

As you read through the stories that follow, you will join me in fond remembrances of the trees and cherished traditions that made up Christmas in the Good Old Days.

—Ken Tate

Just Like the Ones I Used to Know

By Melba Holberg

"Everyone dreams of Christmas 'just like the ones I used to know,'" I mumbled to myself as I left the Christmas store with my granddaughter. Trying to answer her questions as we drove home filled me with a longing to give her not only the information, but the spirit as well.

Though we had little to compare with today's decorations, we loved Christmas and it was a very special time in our lives, filled with such wonderful family traditions. When December came we began to make plans.

We searched the pastures and woods for a small tree or bush with enough foliage to decorate for Christmas. We began to save foil gum wrappers, we went to the country to gather pecans for decorations as well as to eat, we saved colored bits of paper and magazine pages, and we thought about Santa.

We dreamed of Santa, we wrote to Santa and we talked of Santa, but we never, *ever* saw him or even a replica of him. He remained to us a real person who came in the night and disappeared before daylight.

Our parents had us rake leaves and grass for the reindeer to eat, and we left cookies and milk for Santa. We didn't *need* to see him. When the grass disappeared and the milk was gone, we knew that he was real, and that he had come and gone in the night, and left all those surprises for us.

Although we spent the whole month dreaming, thinking and planning, we made no actual preparations until Christmas Eve. That day was a busy one, and just as exciting for us as Christmas Day.

© *The Perfect Tree* by John Sloane

We started by cutting down the desired bush or tree and making the decorations. We wrapped the nuts with gum wrappers to make little silver balls, which we stuck among the twigs of the tree. If we had selected a huisach bush, the thorns made a great place to stick the decorations.

Then we began making the chains. We cut strips from colored paper and colored magazine pages and bent them into rings, linking them together to create long chains. Mama made our paste out of flour and water. It was exciting to see who could make the longest chain.

Sometimes, but not often, we made popcorn chains by threading real popcorn on a string. It was hard to put those chains on the tree when we wanted to eat them instead.

Once, while visiting a neighbor, I saw candles on a tree. They were very, very thin, much like the birthday candles we use today. They were stuck in little holders that clipped onto the tree.

After getting our tree up and admiring it, we raked the yard for the reindeer. While all of this activity was going on, Mama was busy making preparations for our Christmas dinner, and most likely she was also making some of our surprises.

Late in the evening, after all the preparations were made, we went to town. Our town had one main street where the dime store awaited with all its lighted glory. We walked up and down in front of that store, the grocery store, the barber shop and the bakery, looking in at the beautifully lighted windows and displays. Everything seemed so bright and so colorful to a family that didn't have electricity.

I was unaware of it then, but now I know that our parents purchased our gifts on Christmas Eve at that little dime store. When we went in, one of them kept us occupied while the other shopped. It never occurred to us to ask for anything because we wanted to think that Santa brought it. But even when our better judgement destroyed the wonderful myth, we were always surprised.

After the little shopping spree, we proceeded across town to the church, where there would be a pageant and a Christmas tree loaded with candy and fruit for everyone. I loved the pageant with the angels, the shepherds, the Wise Men and the Christ Child in the manger. I loved all the beautiful carols, too. We sometimes kept singing them as we returned home. I loved it all.

I never knew about colored Christmas lights until I was 10 or 12 years old, and I did not see them in a home until I was grown. Few people had electricity in my little hometown. The only nightlights we saw were the stars and, now and then, a car light.

The excitement of my first look at Christmas lights is one of the highlights of my life. It happened one Christmas Eve when we were walking home from the church pageant.

Suddenly, the sky was ablaze with colors. We gazed up at a huge tower where the city fathers had surprised the whole town with the magnificent sight. As people gathered around that tower, looking heavenward, the moment became almost ethereal.

We always got a small toy from the store, like a ball, a cap pistol, a slingshot, some jacks, a small doll or a stuffed animal. But Mama made many of our toys from boxes, scraps of paper, fabric and pieces of wood. Some of them were quite nice and some, of course, were easily destroyed, but we never, ever saw them until Christmas morning. The surprise was wonderful. Though our gifts were few in number and mostly homemade and cheap, I can never remember being disappointed.

On Christmas morning we woke before dawn, lit the kerosene lamp and gathered around the tree to exclaim and compare as the aromas of apples, oranges and kerosene permeated the room. To this very day, I get that same feeling when I smell those odors mingled together. Sometimes I burn my lamps at Christmas just to recapture that wonderful spirit of childhood.

I know my children have loved the Christmas season and I know my grandchildren enjoy it, too. My fondest wish is that they will want to hold on to their own memories as I have done. ✳

A "Chair Christmas"

By Clarice L. Moon

I don't suppose most people have been fortunate enough to have a "chair Christmas." It was a custom handed down from my grandmother, Lurana E. Taylor, who homesteaded on the Nebraska prairies. As there was no wood there to build a home, she lived in a soddy.

When Christmas came around, there were no fireplaces or Christmas trees, so she used a kitchen chair to anchor her stocking. Santa wasn't a bit bashful about leaving gifts in stockings, even if they were pinned to the back of a chair.

One of the gifts she found in her stocking and kept for years was a handcarved jumping jack. It had been made by her older brother.

When my older brother and I celebrated the first Christmas I remember, we were living on a farm in Iowa. Some homes had Christmas trees with candles for lights. But they were expensive, and apt to go up in a puff of smoke. Needless to say, we did not have a tree.

Mother got us ready for bed on Christmas Eve, rubbing us good with warm skunk oil (no, it didn't smell), and then putting on our warm sleepers. Then, the long, black stockings that we wore tucked over our long underwear were pinned up on the chair.

Carrying a kerosene lamp, Mother took us upstairs. We crawled into our cold beds and pulled the patchwork quilts over our heads to warm up. Then Mother went back downstairs with the light. We settled down to listen for reindeer scraping on the roof and dropped off to sleep.

On Christmas morning we were up before daylight. Mother lit the lamp while Dad stocked chunks in the round oak stove.

We spent the morning with our toys. Our stockings bulged with candy, filberts and English walnuts, and each had an orange in the toe. It was the only orange we ever had.

On the chair sat a doll for me. It was a plain, simple doll with a painted face and hair, but to me it was beautiful. It couldn't walk, talk, wet, dance or burp. I couldn't dye its hair, paint its face or give it a bath. Nevertheless, I enjoyed hours of play with it. Sometimes Grandmother made extra dresses and pieced a tiny doll quilt for me.

Besides a doll, I usually got a game like checkers or dominoes, a book like Robert Louis Stevenson's *A Child's Garden of Verses*, and mittens knitted by Grandmother.

My brother found a marble game called Handy Andy. He usually got one every Christmas and it lasted him about a year. He also got a contraption that looked like a tin can, and when he rolled it away from him, it came back. It mystified us. He got *Billy Whiskers* books and Old Maid cards besides his stocking full of loot and new mittens from Grandmother.

By the time we moved to Wisconsin, there were four more children who had been born in Iowa. Two more brothers and a sister were born in Wisconsin.

It was in Wisconsin that we had our first Christmas tree. Now everyone has a tree, and one's gifts are limited only by one's pocketbook. But nothing can be quite as satisfying for me as my "chair Christmas" of long ago. ❋

The Little Church

By K.C. Butterworth

The Christmas I remember most fondly was in 1947, when I was 7 years old. As 7 year olds do, I had waited all year for Christmas. Little did I know that it would be unlike any other Christmas, before or after.

My family went to a little church, and the people who went there didn't have a lot of money. But what was lacking in money was made up in love. Whenever someone was sick, injured or had a new baby, the ladies brought food, kept their homes running and did whatever was needed until they could get back on their feet. Visiting dignitaries always said, "You people are poor in worldly goods, but you are rich in the spirit." And it was true. As a child, however, I used to wonder what it would be like to be rich in worldly goods, and not quite so rich in spirit.

That year was filled with anticipation about the upcoming Christmas program. The congregation was waiting to see how the new minister would handle the program. Each year, Santa Claus arrived at the end of the program and different ministers handled this in different ways. Some played down Santa's part quite a bit, and some allowed him to play a bigger role in the events. This year we would find out how the new minister felt about the matter.

A large tree always was placed in the church hall, and everyone donated their most prized ornaments to decorate it. Many of the members helped with the preparations, and as Christmas drew near, the excitement grew.

Finally, the day arrived! The congregation filed into the hall for the program. I managed to sit close to the front, so the scent from the tree added to my enjoyment of the occasion.

The program consisted of musical numbers, congregational singing of carols and a reading of *The Night Before Christmas*. Throughout the evening, the new minister worked up the crowd—especially the youngsters—into a frenzy of excitement. As he introduced each number, he interrupted with, "Do I hear sleigh bells?" or, "Was that a 'Ho, ho, ho!' I heard?" Then he walked to the door, opened it and peered out, apparently looking for Santa. By the time the program finally concluded, all the other children and I were wide-eyed with excitement.

And then, Santa rushed through the door, carrying a big bag of gifts! A cheer arose to greet him. Soon I was in line, awaiting my turn to sit on Santa's lap, tell him what I wanted for Christmas, and get my Christmas stocking. Our stockings were the old-fashioned kind, with holes in them, and were filled with hard candy, nuts and fruit. How special I felt, taking that stocking home, and knowing that Santa had filled it especially for me!

That unusual Christmas program was fondly remembered for years to come. There never was another like it. By the next Christmas, the new minister had left, replaced by yet another new minister.

In the many years that have come and gone since then, there have been many changes. Quite a few ministers have come and gone. The congregation outgrew the little church and built a big, beautiful sanctuary. The original little church is still standing, but now it is a lodge hall.

The members have also changed. They are more prosperous, and enjoy a more affluent lifestyle. Visiting dignitaries now say, "You are very blessed to have the money to pay for such a beautiful church."

Visiting dignitaries always said, "You people are poor in worldly goods, but you are rich in the spirit." And it was true.

Now I sometimes think about how wonderful it would be to go back to that little church—and to feel the security and warmth in the love that was there. I often feel it might be nice to be a little poorer in worldly goods but richer in the spirit.

But then I realize that He whose birth Christmas celebrates gave the answer when He said, "Feed the hungry, clothe the naked, care for the sick." And I understand that all the wonderful things I gained in the little church are still with me. All I need to do is express them, by following His divine example.

And when I'm alone, feeling a little lonely—and perhaps a little sad—it's all still there: the little church, the new minister, Santa with his big bag of gifts, and all the feelings of warmth and security. All I need do is close my eyes, think very hard, and I can still see it all. ✳

Christmas Eve Then & Now

By Opal F. Husted

The Christmas Eves of the 1920s at the home of my grandparents, Flo and Let, were happy times. Their 13 children gathered to celebrate, and with crackers and soup, no one was hungry for long. Kerosene lamps sent ghostly shadows across the rooms as the grandchildren waited with great anticipation for old Santa's visit.

But first things first. The married children and their families had arrived during the afternoon, yelling, "Christmas Eve gift!" to everyone. All lived within 10 miles of their parents' home. Several families traveled along the crusty, frozen, Missouri dirt roads in buggies or wagons, covering up with heavy blankets to keep warm. Only a few had automobiles, and they drained their radiators of water when they arrived, as everyone spent the night. Horses had to be unharnessed and made comfortable, too.

The house was toasty warm thanks to the Round Oak stove and the kitchen range. The bedrooms were cold but we didn't worry about that; the children crowded into the beds, sleeping crossways, and they had a lot of body heat.

My two sisters, Charlotte and Vera Dale, and I got reacquainted with our first cousins quickly. Then the happy play noise began.

Soup time came next—a choice of oyster or vegetable in the big pots, with potato for those with squeamish stomachs. The men were served at the room-length table first, while children of assorted sizes sat with their filled bowls on the freshly scrubbed, bare, wooden floor. With all the chatter and laughter coming from the women washing dishes in the kitchen, you wouldn't have thought they minded eating last.

After clearing away the food, most of the group waited in the living room for the program to begin. The treks to the outhouse began, too, as the soup and cold well water took effect.

At last—the program. All the children who were old enough gave a Christmas recitation or nursery rhyme. The whole group sang old-time carols as my mother played the pump organ. The Husteds were never too musical, but she drowned out some of the sour notes.

As the last song ended, sleigh bells sounded outside the front door and someone let Santa in. I was thrilled! I can still feel how my hair stood on end as he handed me new mittens. Amid all the laughing and talking, hardly anyone noticed that the adults didn't receive presents.

The years sped along, bringing changes and new generations. The group became a little more prosperous in the 1940s. They met at my parents' home then, and I helped get the basement table ready to help accommodate the crowd. As many as 70 had drawn names earlier, with the price limit set at $1 per gift.

The play was real work now, too, as was the cleanup afterward. Snow was stamped across the new carpet, a dropped cigarette burned a hole in the kitchen linoleum and greasy popcorn was tracked through the house.

Later, for several years, the crowd met at the nearby Martinstown Community Building. There the cleanup was much easier.

Now only two of the original 13 children, Hattie and Earl, are still living. There have been six generations that I remember: my grandparents, parents, first cousins, their children, grandchildren and a few great-grandchildren. For the past few years we have been meeting at Cousin Vivian's new, underground house with all the modern conveniences. We have Christmas grab bags for all. Still, many of the family traditions remain. When we all enter the house, we still yell, "Christmas Eve gift!" We still eat soup and sing songs, and Santa still comes. Nostalgia fills the air as we remember the past. As we eat and visit, we are proud to still be a close-knit family. ✳

A Reindeer Christmas Party

By Violet M. Appeman

"Let's have another Reindeer Party this Christmas!" someone would say who had been to one out at our farm on the North Dakota prairie. That was before the days of radio or television, when we made our own fun. We'd whip up a party at the drop of a hat, and a Reindeer Party was one of them each Christmas.

A Reindeer Party required at least eight persons. Each was named for one of Santa's tiny reindeer—Dasher, Dancer, Prancer, Vixen, Comet, Cupid, Donner, Blitzen—and wore his name on a brown paper headband adorned with a set of stiff cardboard antlers. If there were more than eight guests, we just added Santa's Helping Elves, and a Mr. and Mrs. Santa; Rudolph the Red-Nosed Reindeer might also join us.

One year we planned the Reindeer Party so hastily that we didn't have time to make cardboard antlers. Instead, we just created bibs from white crepe paper, lettered the names on them with red crayon, and tied the bibs around the neck with red and green drawstrings. (That was the year we had a spaghetti dinner, so the bibs came handy.)

We always served two things at our Christmas parties: cider, hot and spiced, and sauerkraut. We cooked the kraut the day before "to bring up the taste," adding caraway seeds. We'd also have mashed potatoes and creamed onions, and peppermint pie for dessert.

The first stunt upon the arrival of the guests was to pin on Santa's whiskers. A big, hand-sketched face of Santa was fastened up on the wall. Each guest was given a tuft of cotton and a pin; then he was blindfolded, turned around three times, and told to reach out and fasten on Santa's beard. The whiskers coming nearest the chin got a prize, and the ones farthest away a booby prize.

We played games at the table while the table was cleared between the main course and dessert. Santa had left presents for everybody, wrapped but without names on them. We placed these on a big tray, which was then passed rapidly around the table while a lively tune was played on the piano. Each guest selected a package as the tray came around, but could put it back on and exchange it for another, as sometimes the tray whizzed around four times before the piano player stopped abruptly. Then each kept what he held. After opening the gifts, all could exchange to suit their liking. It was a lot of fun.

After dessert we "read our Christmas mail." Each was given a sheet of paper on which was copied a version of the then-popular Tall Tales, or Fish Stories, or Windies, or Paul Bunyan yarns. These were read aloud, and a prize went to the one getting the biggest applause, while a consolation prize was awarded to the corniest. We ended by just giving both the same prize— "Nuts to You," a small box of shelled nuts.

To help "settle our dinners" we played Fruit Basket Upset, adapted for the occasion by using the reindeers' names instead of names of fruit. All except the one who was "It" sat in a circle of chairs. "It" stood in the center and called out the names of two reindeer, who bolted to exchange places. Meanwhile, "It" tried to steal one of their chairs. The one left standing was then "It," and called out the names of two more reindeer, the farther apart the better. But if he said, "Santa's sleigh upsets!" everybody leaped up and changed seats, while "It" watched for a chance to nab a chair for himself.

We also played Hide the Thimble, Post Office and many other oldies. One year we featured a "mixed quartet." We hung an old sheet over a doorway and cut four holes in it at different heights, through which four singers thrust their faces. One knelt behind the curtain, one stood on a high stool, and the other two clowned at in-between levels.

The "producer" of this famous mixed quartet gave an elaborate introduction: "La-deez and Gen-men! It is now our pleasure to present to you one of the greatest musical productions you will ever hear on the planet! Once you hear them, you will be forced to agree—so may I present to you, the World-Famous Mixed Quartet!"

At his signal, each blurted out a different Christmas song at the top of his lungs. No one as ever able to carry his song further than several _rs. One by one, the faces disappeared from the _les in the curtain. Just once the bass singer, pur-_e-cheeked, managed to keep on chanting, "'Tis _e season to be jolly, fa-la-la-la-la, la-la-la-LA!"

At the close of the party came the time to _deem the forfeits—"fines" usually issued as _atches levied for slipping up by using the _artygoers' right names instead of reindeer _ames. Stunts were written on cards, one for _ach "fine." We did whatever stunt was described: imitating a dog burying a bone, riding a bike, imitating Sherlock Holmes searching for a clue, an eavesdropper peeping through a key-hole, cackling like a hen over a newly laid egg, crowing like a rooster at sunrise, and so forth.

By then we usually felt like sitting around contentedly to listen to a good reader present *'Twas the Night Before Christmas*. We always ended by singing carols—a fitting close to another evening of fun, as we gave true Christmas spirit its rightful place. ❊

Christmas Sights, Smells & Sounds

By Melba Eyler

I'll never forget our Christmas trees in St. Louis. The ceilings in the old brick house were very high, made especially, it seemed, to accommodate our big Christmas trees with the scenic village on its raised platform. Ours was no little shrub set in a stand or placed in a tub. It was a tree that reached to the ceiling, and it lorded over the ever-changing and interesting activities that were going on in the little village below it.

Our tree was awash in the glow of flickering lights from many candles, each placed in a tiny holder that clamped onto the tip of a branch. They were carefully arranged so that the branches above did not become torches.

The platform scene beneath the tree's boughs could hold a child's interest for hours. We watched the bustling little train scooting around and around on its track. It whisked through a tunnel in a mountain built at the back of the village.

We watched the little, blue frosted windmill that turned somehow, and we looked into the little houses and stores. Most intriguing was the tavern, complete with lights and people inside. I remember how the small customers stood at the bar, resting their feet on a footrail. We were entranced by it.

We watched, fascinated, as tiny ice skaters glided over a pond made from a mirror set into a snow scene.

Little lamp posts helped light the village. People were placed on walkways, and small automobiles and horse-drawn wagons joined the activity. Groups of children played with their sleds. There even was a scaled-to-size snowman, complete with top hat and scarf.

All our Christmases in St. Louis were wonderful, but one Christmas Eve in particular stands out in memory.

Santa had just left. We knew he had gone, for when he left, he blew horns, and we saw him as he slipped out the front door (and he wasn't our father, either, for *he* was there with us). Then we burst through the sliding doors and the portieres, into the living room. It was like stepping into a living Christmas card.

Each year when we first saw the lighted tree, it was like seeing it for the very first time. It made my breath go out in a puff, and it took a moment to get it all back. Then, quickly, our eyes darted to see what Santa had left.

This particular Christmas he had been unusually generous. There was a good-size, brass doll bed (made by my father). It had a rounded head and base formed with set-in brass rods. Reclining on the bed were two dolls completely dressed and prepared for outdoor fun. My mother had crocheted little outfits— coats, bonnets and shoes—for each of them.

On the new, shining sled sat two teddy bears, each wearing a stocking hat. A doll swing, the kind with facing seats, held two more sophisticated dolls.

There were Christmas smells, as well—the aromas of baked cookies, which were always stored in big white bags (probably flour bags). The plum puddings and fruitcakes were baked days ahead, and so were the *pfeffernusse* and the anise cookies, which were hard to bite if we tried to eat them too soon.

Then there was the wonderful scent of the tree, of pitch and pungent pine. But most remembered, after the candles were blown out, was the aroma of the warm wax mingled with an acrid, smoky smell.

There were sounds of Christmas, too: carolers, their footsteps crunching in the snow, their voices floating on the cold, crisp air like tinkling icicles. There were church bells ringing, and the sounds of laughter and merriment.

It was all there, and it still is, in memory— the sights and smells and sounds of Christmases to be remembered. ❄

Christmas Caroling by Charles Berger, House of White Birches nostalgia archives

CHARLES BERGER

John Slobodnik

Those Wonderful Christmas Cookies

By Ginger K. Nelson

"This feels like it's going to be really good to work with this year," my aunt says, squishing cookie dough through her fingers until the consistency feels right.

I dip my finger in and taste. "Better than ever. I think I'd like a bit more of a lemony taste." My mother squeezes fresh lemon over the dough. "Perfect," I proclaim. We are ready to roll—literally.

Rolling pins, bags of flour, a pile of Christmas cookie cutters and several assorted baking tins line my kitchen table. My mother tends the oven, making sure each delectable cookie is baked just right. The long sheets of waxed paper that line the counters fill rapidly with Santas, stars, sleighs and bells delicately brushed with egg white and sprinkled with colored sugar. My aunt and I roll and cut, reminding my mother when "they smell done."

Baking Christmas cookies together is one way that we carry on the traditions of my Hungarian grandmother. Using a kitchen scale and her senses along with her good sense, Grandmother produced some wonderful cookies. Now, when we use her recipes, the cookies' cinnamony and lemony fragrances remind me each year of her. As we bake her Christmas cookies, I also recall cuddling in her ample folds, gently fingering her soft, white, carefully pulled-back hair, and watching in awe as her hands swiftly and perfectly shaped each cookie.

Now I watch my 83-year-old mother and my 79-year-old aunt deftly knead and roll cookie dough, while they recite the same stories each year.

"Remember how Mama's cookies were always the same? And how she could roll them so thin without breaking them?" Each year I take pictures of our cookie-baking sessions to imprint these memories on my mind. And I wonder if someday my grandchildren will delight in helping me make those wonderful Christmas cookies, which will turn into memories each year during the holidays.

> *"Remember how Mama's cookies were always the same? And how she could roll them so thin without breaking them?"*

❄ ❄ ❄ ❄ ❄

For all the following cookies, set out ingredients until they reach room temperature so that they are easily mixed. Blend together by hand according to instructions in each recipe. Shape dough into large balls, cover with waxed paper, and refrigerate. The chilling will enable you to roll out the dough more easily. Chilling time should be approximately 1 hour, or until easy to handle.

When ready to begin, remove one ball of dough at a time, leaving the remainder in the refrigerator. Roll out according to specific instructions. Because most of the recipes require only the egg yolks, save the whites for the vanilla *kipfle* and refrigerate the remainder in a small container.

Use these extra egg whites as a topping for all but the vanilla *kipfle*. Beat the whites with a fork and brush lightly across the tops of the cookies before adding Christmas sprinkles. This makes a shiny surface and keeps the decorations from falling off.

Christmas Cookie Time by John Slobodnik, House of White Birches nostalgia archives

All cookies are baked on ungreased cookie sheets. (The new insulated cookie sheets, however, are best coated lightly with vegetable spray or as directions indicate.) After baking, set aside until completely cooled before placing in storage containers.

Thin Butter Cookies

½ pound sweet butter
2½ cups flour
Grated peel of ½ lemon
1½ cups confectioners' sugar
3 eggs

Mix all ingredients until smooth. Roll out on floured board and cut with desired cookie cutters. Decorate and bake in a 350-degree oven for about 10 minutes, or until lightly browned. Makes 4 dozen.

Linza Cookies

4½ cups flour
1 cup margarine
2 cups sugar
Pinch of salt
2 whole eggs *plus* 1 egg yolk
1 teaspoon baking soda
Juice of 1 lemon

Mix flour, margarine, sugar and salt with hands. Make a well in middle and put in eggs, egg yolk, baking soda and lemon juice.

Mix well. Roll on floured board to about ¼ inch in thickness. Shape with cookie cutters and decorate. Bake in a 350-degree oven for about 10 minutes, or until lightly browned. Makes 4 dozen.

Cinnamon Cookies

4½ cups flour
1 pound sweet butter
1 cup confectioners' sugar
2 whole eggs
1 teaspoon baking powder
½ cup (or more) cinnamon

Mix all ingredients well. Roll out on floured board; cut with desired cookie cutters; decorate. Bake in a 350-degree oven for about 10 minutes, or until done. Makes 5 dozen.

Cream Cheese Cookies

½ pound cream cheese
1 cup confectioners' sugar
Grated peel of ½ lemon
½ teaspoon baking powder
½ pound sweet butter
1 egg yolk
2 cups flour
¼ teaspoon salt

Mix all ingredients, shape into balls and refrigerate for *several hours*. Roll about ½ inch thick on floured board. Bake at 350 degrees for about 20 minutes or until lightly browned. Makes 5 dozen.

Vanilla *Kipfle*

A few days prior to baking, place a vanilla bean in each box of confectioners' sugar you will use to bake and to roll to give added flavor. Use 2–3 boxes. When ready to coat baked cookies, place some of the vanilla sugar in a large container; a roasting pan works well. Roll cookies in flavored confectioners' sugar to coat.

3½ cups flour
1 cup ground almonds
3 teaspoons vanilla
½ pound sweet butter
¼ cup egg whites (add more if dough is crumbly)
1¾ cups confectioners' sugar, plus additional for coating baked cookies

Mix all ingredients *except the confectioners' sugar for coating* until dough comes together in one lump and pulls away from sides of the bowl. Using your hands, form a log as thick as your finger. Cut into 3-inch pieces with a sharp knife and shape each into a horseshoe. Bake in 350-degree oven for 12–15 minutes, or until lightly browned. Remove from pan and immediately place in large container with additional confectioners' sugar (remove vanilla bean). Coat with confectioners' sugar, then remove to cool. Makes 5 dozen. ❋

Christmas Pound Fruitcake

By Katherine Durack

Many years ago, my Grandmother Lane clipped and saved a recipe for "Christmas Pound Fruitcake." As a working mother during and after World War II, she apparently never had the opportunity to bake the cake, but the clipping lay preserved among her papers for many years.

When Grandmother Lane passed away, my mother found the recipe and passed it along to me. As a tradition I've made the fruitcake almost every year since. I am among those who don't usually care for fruitcake, but this recipe, with its tempting assortment of nuts and spices, is always well-received.

Here's the recipe as it originally appeared.
1 pound citron
1 pound almonds
1 pound currants
2 pounds raisins
1 pound flour
1 pound butter
1 pound sugar
9 eggs
4 teaspoons baking powder
6 teaspoons cinnamon
4 teaspoons cloves
4½ teaspoons mace
3½ teaspoons nutmeg
3½ teaspoons allspice
2 tablespoons salt
1 cup grape juice

Combine the fruits and nuts. Add enough of the flour to separate. Sift together remaining flour, baking powder, spices and salt. Cream butter and sugar. Add egg yolks, dry ingredients and liquids alternately.

Fold in well-beaten egg whites. Pour into pans lined with greased paper. Bake in slow oven 2–3 hours or steam 4–5 hours and place in very slow oven 1 hour to dry off. Makes 2 or more cakes.

I vary the combination of fruit and nuts each year (though always keeping the total at 5 pounds), according to the price and availability of dried fruit and nuts at my local whole-foods store. Popular versions have included chopped figs, dates, dried apples, dried pineapple and pecans.

Being a somewhat lazy cook, I have also added the eggs unseparated, with no apparent effect on the final product.

According to one of my cookbooks, a "slow oven" is roughly equivalent to 300 degrees, and that's worked for me. Some years, I've drizzled a runny icing made with powdered sugar, water and sometimes a touch of almond extract across the tops of the cooled fruitcakes.

This recipe will require your very largest bowl, but it will make truly delicious fruitcake for you, your family and your friends. ❉

DICK SARGENT

A Mousetrap Christmas

By Gale Ann Van Buren

Every family has special traditions and stories, as well as ornaments, decorations, trims and goodies that they bring out at the start of the holiday season. My family is no different. One of our stories never fails to bring giggles of delight from nieces and nephews, hearty laughs from friends, a knowing smile from my mother and a blush of remembered guilt to my own face. Looking back, though, I can admit that I probably deserved it. And I, too, can laugh about my Mousetrap Christmas.

Even as a very young child, I was a snoop. I peeked into the "gift closet," checked catalog orders, rattled packages and, when all else failed, I resorted to bribery. I just could not wait! The suspense would surely kill me, or so I thought. My mother hoped that I would outgrow this trait, but she hoped in vain. Rather than outgrow it, the older I got, the worse my "sickness" became.

One day, my mother decided that the time had come to call in the "snoop breakers" and teach me a lesson. Being fair, she warned me several times before "it" happened.

Our closets were separated by a very thin wall, and through a small accident, an umbrella had punched a hole in it. That hole was just the right size for a hand, and from the safety of my own closet, I could reach through to pat and punch, pull and peek to my heart's delight. And oh, how my snoopy heart delighted!

One day my mother and grandmother brought the most interesting-looking packages into the house. They warned us that they were none of our business, and their warning was sufficient for my brother, Mike, and sister, Susan. But to a snoop like me, it was a challenge to be met.

Quietly I crept into my special place while the rest of the family went about their business. I dropped to my knees and reached into the neighboring closet. Then my exploring fingers touched a small wooden object, unwrapped but so tiny. My fingers traveled the length, and I was totally perplexed—then suddenly, with a snap, I knew what it was.

I screamed and jumped to my feet, knocking clothes down. I retreated from the closet, pain stabbing my fingers.

My family came on the run, and there I stood, a mousetrap extending from three fingers and a sheepish look on my face.

"Do you like your little surprise, Gale?" Mom asked, while the rest of the family hooted and laughed.

"Merry Christmas, Snoop," she said, smiling, as she removed it. "And by the way, you will never know where one of these will be, so you'd better quit snooping." That trap had caught its prey—not a rat, to be sure, but a snoop. The bait, a closetful of assorted packages, bundles and surprises, had lured a real prize.

Don't tell my mom, but sometimes the urge still comes over me and I can't resist one little snoop for old times' sake. But it isn't as much fun now since I always wear heavy work gloves … just in case. ❋

> *Even as a very young child, I was a snoop. I peeked into the "gift closet," checked catalog orders, rattled packages and, when all else failed, I resorted to bribery.*

Christmas Ornaments

By Gloria Bundy

It was Epiphany, Jan. 6, the day that traditionally the Wise Men came to the stable to see the Christ Child. Christmas was over for another year. It was time to take down the decorations, store them for next year and go on with our lives.

As I took the ornaments off the tree I was reminded of family members not with us anymore—of Christmases past. Many of my ornaments have memories associated with them and have been on our Christmas trees for generations.

I took the solid blue ornament off and held it to look at its workmanship again, as I do every Christmas. Grandpa brought it with his belongings when he came to live with our family after Grandma died in 1941. It is solid, not hollow like many modern ornaments, and the manger is embedded in the mold of the ornament.

A solid ornament meant to last, I thought. *It reminds me of Grandpa, a solid, sturdy German who always built and worked to make everything of lasting value.* The ornament hung on the trees in his boyhood home on the farm in the 1860s and 1870s.

When I was a child, Dad had a country store. On the day after Thanksgiving, he and Mom set up the display of Christmas merchandise. An old man from a nearby farm came each year and brought a cedar tree that they decorated after the store closed at 7 o'clock. Among the items for sale were Christmas tree ornaments, and among the ornaments I took off my tree this year were ornaments from Dad's store.

Those ornaments were very fragile, made of thin, glasslike material that broke easily. I thought of how carefully Dad and Mom handled the ornaments when someone bought one. Dad would wrap each in a piece of newspaper, then carefully put it in a box. Dad would hand the box to the purchaser and say, "They are 5 cents apiece."

Time passed. World War II was upon us. No longer were beautiful colored ornaments available; now they were plastic. We purchased a few new ones and I took down a little red boot, a little red house and a little red bell. Dad no longer had the store, but he helped decorate our tree at home.

Mom, Grandpa and I all shared in the joy of putting up the tree. But something was not right. We thought of so many of "our boys" fighting and dying in foreign lands, languishing in prison camps and sent home because of injuries. My own husband was in far-off Okinawa. Finally the war was over and my husband came home.

During the Korean War we settled into our home on the farm where Grandpa had grown up. A few days before Christmas we walked out into the woods and cut our own little cedar tree. We put it into a stand and set it in our living room, then went shopping for ornaments.

That year, about all that was available were plastic foam ones in different shapes—bells, snowballs and stars, among others. And they were all white. *A far cry,* I thought, *from the colorful ones Dad once sold in his store.* But we bought enough for our little tree, and after we hung them and strung the electric lights, we thought it looked pretty. After all, it was our first tree together. When I took these ornaments off my tree this year, I noticed that they were all there; not much can happen to a plastic foam ornament!

I held the ones our oldest son had created with Mom when he was little. They had decorated some of our plain, white, plastic foam ornaments with Christmas seals and ribbons. My thoughts went back more than 50 years, when he and Mom had created all kinds of decorations for the Christmas season, including a paper chain made of construction paper. As I took down what remains of that chain after all these years, I carefully folded it and put it in a bag; maybe it can hang on the tree one more year.

I held the doll for a moment when I took it off the tree. I remembered how I had always admired it when I was a child and it had hung on Aunt Leona's tree. And then, one year, she took it off her tree and gave it to me. It wore a

Family Fun Trimming the Tree by Charles Berger, House of White Birches nostalgia archives

skirt of tiny feathers. I thought it was a real treasure. The feathers began to fall off long ago, but the doll hangs on my tree every year.

I took down the celluloid doll that my grandma and grandpa had displayed on their tree before 1941. Grandma, who had dressed it in a tiny dress, didn't forget to sew a tiny pair of matching bloomers for it.

Today, when craft shops are flourishing, people make ornaments out of felt decorated with sequined designs, and crochet covers to fit over shiny, colored balls. I recently bought a few

and I have received some others as gifts.

This year I was elated to find a gift shop with a Christmas tree bearing molded ornaments exactly like the ones Dad sold when I was a child. Made in Germany, they no longer cost 5 cents apiece. But I bought four of them anyway.

I especially wanted the colorful bird with the white plastic tail, which clips onto a branch. Dad, who disliked changes so much, would smile to see the bird perched on my tree, which his great-granddaughter Catherine and I cut down in the woods our behind the barn. ❄

The First Lighted Christmas Tree

By Harriet E. Gowey

The first Christmas trees I remember were candlelit. But when I think of our first lighted Christmas tree, I'm not talking about those, though my memories of them are very vivid.

When I was a child, my family's trees were never candlelit, for the dangerous practice resulted in many fires and my father would never allow it. But a large family who lived across the street from us always had a candlelit tree. Each of their many children was allowed to bring a little friend on Christmas night to witness their candle-lighting ceremony.

I was always chosen by one of the little girls, and so I got to sit on the floor in the living room, clasping my Christmas doll in my arms, while the father lit the wax tapers on their 10-foot tree with the special taper used for lighting gaslights. When the last candle was lit, he would take his position in the dining-room doorway, a pail of water on each side in case the tree should catch fire.

The mother took her place at the piano and played Christmas carols as long as the candles burned. All the children sang, and I am sure none of us ever forgot those bright moments. I never have, although all this was 70 years ago!

The other memorable Christmas tree was from some time later, in the Hotel Bellevue-Stratford in downtown Philadelphia. It was my father's yearly custom to take Mother and me into Philadelphia one evening just before Christmas to see the lighted stores and do a little last-minute shopping. We took a local train, known as the Redding Road, from our suburban home into the city, and as part of the fun, we always stopped somewhere for ice cream and cake.

In 1905, he took us to the Bellevue-Stratford for our refreshments, for he knew about their lighted trees. They were not real trees, but were made to resemble them by winding the pillars in the hotel dining room with ropes of greenery intertwined with strands of small, colored lights. The effect was very pretty, and they attracted many guests to the hotel, for these were the first tiny colored lights that anyone in Philadelphia had seen.

The first such lights that we had on our own home tree were bought for the Christmas of 1911, after we had moved to Denver, Colo. My mother protested their purchase as an extravagance, for the lights cost $8 for a string of only eight little globes. But I was delighted and got a real thrill out of admitting the many strangers who came to our door and asked to see "the tree with the electric lights" they had heard about.

The tiny globes were different from today's lights. They ended in a sharp point and were very durable. In fact, I still have two globes from that early string—and they still light!

This tree, my first "all-electric" one, still glows in my memory. It can never be displaced by the trees I have nowadays, whose beauty is enjoyed by the married children and grandchildren who gather around them. ❋

Blue Junk

By Audrey Theurer

That was the year—the year we divided all the trimmings among the married children and had a beautifully planned symbol of the season.

"Let's have a flocked tree," my husband said, "trimmed in all one color, just for fun."

"What color?" asked a new daughter-in-law. She was startled at the laughter from all my sons.

"It will have to be blue," one said, "or she won't play."

"She won't have a tree she can't hang her blue junk on," another son explained, and while the girls waited expectantly, I brought forth the small box that holds the two tarnished and faded blue ornaments. I could not get these young people to realize that these small globes hold all the Christmases that one middle-aged lady ever had.

In 1935, at the old Main Street grade school in Dallas, we placed a bare fir tree in the corner of the first-grade room. Each child could bring two decorations from home, Mrs. Ruth explained. That way, the tree would be decorated for our Christmas party. It would have to be the grandest tree in the whole school, because we were the smallest children, and because the principal would be there, and because we would be excused an hour early.

That is exactly the way I remember it. That tree standing bare, then trimmed, is clear to me yet—even though I can't for the life of me remember the party or the principal.

All the way home, I worried. Our Christmas things were still packed away, way up in the attic, and Dad couldn't get them down, for he was working away from home. All that long weekend we waited, just in case he might get home—but he didn't. I cried myself to sleep under the covers that Sunday night; the last thought I had was a vision of that bare tree.

In the way of mothers, Mom followed me out the door the next morning and put our movie dime into my mitten. (Mom and all four of us kids went to the movie for 10 cents on Wednesday night if Dad wasn't home.) She told me to stop at the variety store on my way to school and pick out two 5-cent decorations. If Dad got home, we would have movie money; and if he didn't, we could stay home and pop corn.

It seemed that there were at least 10 million jewel-like objects on the counter of the store, and the largest selections were marked 5 cents each. Bedded deep in loose straw, the ornaments were in all shapes, sizes and colors.

I was so excited that goose bumps marched up my arms and down my legs. Clutching the dime tightly, I walked up and down that aisle on tiptoe at least a dozen times. It was the very first money I ever had been given to spend and I wasn't going to make a mistake.

The first ornament I chose was a cluster of grapes about 2 inches long, the shades of blue blending into a serious color that glittered when turned to the light. Diamond rings, new babies and expensive cars have passed through my hands since then, but I have never had the same feeling of complete surrender.

The second bauble was chosen quickly when the school bell rang three blocks away. It was pale blue and had a white design of mistletoe.

Those ornaments winked at me from the branches of "our tree" all that week. After the party, I carried them home carefully, one in each hand. They were the only new trims on our Christmas tree in that Depression year. That Christmas, those ornaments on our tree made up for the long brown cotton stockings I received instead of the white ones I had my heart set on.

The blue ornaments followed me through my childhood. They were two of only four that survived the year the Christmas tree fell over "all by itself" in a room with five boisterous children. During my teens they were not replaced because of a war that made buying new ones impossible.

Later, when we lived in Philomath and were planning the Christmas tree for our first son, Dad helped me unpack all the trimmings at his house in Portland after a full Thanksgiving dinner.

"Is *that* what I got all this stuff down for?"

he stormed when I found what I wanted at the bottom of the last box. "If you need new stuff, I'll get you some!" he huffed, reaching for his billfold. I tried to explain that those ancient blue ornaments held Dallas, Clatskanie, brown stockings, eggnog, a first kiss, giggles and many other things. He listened and chewed his cigar, but I'm not sure he really understood.

I haven't tried to explain it again.

There have been 25 Christmases since then, shared with family, three sons, new daughters, and this year, a new grandson. The flocked white tree trimmed in blue will be on the table, out of reach of yet another child, and in its uppermost branches will be two of the most beautiful blue trinkets in the entire world. ✻

The Last Christmas Tree

By Marion Schoeberlein

We had no way of knowing it was Grandmother's last Christmas. When I was a little girl, Grandma read stories to me by the hour. She taught me the beauty of a cracked teacup, an oddly shaped cloud, a crooked road. I'll always remember her little house with the big willow tree in the back yard.

Because my mother hated picnics, Grandmother took me to all the Sunday School picnics, filling a basket with potato salad, hard-boiled eggs and cheese sandwiches, not to mention the pickles and chocolate cake.

Grandmother was also the most religious woman I ever knew. Her husband had been a minister. His sudden death at 50 made her a widow, but she was never bitter. She went right on, continuing Christmas for us in her little house.

We loved the little tree she decorated with the unique, fragile ornaments from Germany. Her cookies were special, too—mostly anise, rolled out with a rolling pin from Germany. Some were soft, but some were so hard that we had to "dunk" them in coffee for a long time.

Her last Christmas was no different from the others, except that Grandmother looked like a trapped bird, trembling. She wanted to be off, I guess, into heaven. She was 88 years old. We all had noticed how rickety she walked, but she didn't use a cane.

That last Christmas Eve she was with us, everything was as perfect and as beautiful as it had ever been. She must have known that everything old, everything beautiful, was gradually vanishing.

She sat at the table with us, nibbling at her food: chicken, potatoes and gravy, peas and carrots, mince pie. We noticed that she hardly touched it, while we ate as if it were our last meal. Grandmother kept looking at the Christmas tree. Feelings from everywhere must have gathered in her chest. She had known better days with Jesus and wondered if He realized how low she had sunk lately. Loneliness. Of course, none of us knew this.

"Grandma, your hand-crocheted ornaments are prettier than ever," someone said.

"I know. I still wash and starch them every year." The birds and the angel faces and the other ornaments from Germany were as sparkling as ever, too.

Then Grandmother did a strange thing. She got up and went over to her old upright piano and told us to gather around. "I still remember *O Tannenbaum*," she said, and her fingers caressed the old yellow keys in something like the tune. Her eyes shone and she seemed young again as we sang above her whispering piano.

The old bonfire of Christmas had started in her heart. The warm winter sunlight fell on her, shadowing a halo. The fey sprite of Christmas danced in her trembling hands. Then she got up and went over to the tree. "It's more beautiful this year than it's ever been," she said.

Nobody said a word. We wanted this moment to stay with us forever: our eggshell-fragile old grandmother, giving us her blessing in her own way. At that moment, Grandmother looked to me like the most beautiful woman who ever lived.

Her tree seemed to come alive. The pine branches glistened, and the scent of their needles was suddenly intense. Beneath the tree stood the tiny manger her husband had carved in his spare time, so long ago.

Grandmother knew it was her moment. Her tree. Her Christmas. Her manger. Everything else was straw. ✳

Grandma's Favorite Gift by Charles Berger, House of White Birches nostalgia archives

Christmas at Grandma's

Chapter Five

When I was a youngster, we always cut two Christmas trees—one for us and one for Grandma.

Dennis, Donna and I must have been the luckiest kids on earth. With our widowed grandmother living only a short walk away, we had the enviable task of helping to choose, cut and decorate two trees and two homes. The only problem was making a difference between those two trees and two homes, keeping individuality for each.

We usually waited until the Sunday afternoon before Christmas to get our trees. The tiny group of us—Daddy, Mama and three kids—went about our yuletide tasks trooping to the beat of *O Come All Ye Faithful* and *O Little Town of Bethlehem*. Sometimes Grandma Stamps went with us, lending her many years of holiday experience to the whole *Tannenbaum* task.

Both trees were chosen from the wooded acreage just across the road from our home. It was a favorite spot of mine, a rough knoll that sloped gently down to a small meadow. The hollows around the pasture were filled with huge oaks, hickories and glade after glade of evergreens.

Daddy had the job of actually cutting down the tree, but he would take a breather long enough for us upstarts to take a hack or two at it. For a long time I just knew that those cedars were part rubber tree, the way the ax bounced back from each thrust I made. Dennis always seemed to have better luck—but I always figured that it was because he was five years older. The secrets of wood chopping came much later for this awkward left-hander.

For our home, we usually chose a thick, well-rounded cedar. We dragged it back to the house in the crisp, icy December air. I liked the shape of the cedar and the pungent aroma that filled the living room soon after we had trimmed the tree. As we hung tinsel and ornaments, we laughed and sang together, filled with the spirit of the season.

Then it was off to Grandma's with her tree. Many times I remember us getting Grandma Stamps a pine. The pines were sparser of limb, so we had to spend more time planning how to fill the gaps with various Christmas paraphernalia to give Grandma's tree a little more "body." She always thought the job we grandchildren did was perfect in every way; then again, I think we could have done anything short of burning down the tree with the house around it, and the job likewise would have been "perfect" to Grandma.

Finally, it was back to our house for one last round of carols before bedtime. Singing songs of my Maker and His Son filled me with as much warmth as that old wood stove glowing in the corner. Cutting two Christmas trees always seemed to bring twice the fun, twice the love, twice the joy to our little world. Having Grandma so close doubled all of that again. That manifold portion of fun, love and joy always reassured me that at least one season out of the year would be filled with "peace on earth, goodwill toward men." That was what Christmas at Grandma's was all about back in the Good Old Days.

—*Ken Tate*

Stringing Popcorn With Grandma by John Slobodnik, House of White Birches nostalgia archives

The Christmas That Didn't Flop!

By Gertrude R. Lobrot

This Christmas of 1916 was going to be a flop, at least in the eyes of the children of our family. Every other Christmas had been highlighted by a 2 o'clock dinner at Grandpa and Grandma's. After dinner, the family gathered in a circle according to age and gave, received and opened their presents amid the "oohs" and "aahs" of all assembled.

But this year was to be different. Grandpa had died a month before and our parents decided that Grandma was too tired to have a big dinner. I am sure she was, but as kids we couldn't envision Grandma tired. Why, she was *Grandma*!

But no amount of coaxing did any good. We would have our gifts from Santa Claus, Christmas dinner with only our family present, and then in the late afternoon, take the streetcar to Grandma's with our gifts for her.

Christmas morning dawned cold and dreary. A light snow had fallen during the night and the sun could not break through the clouds. But Santa had been most generous. I think he had felt sorry for us because of Grandma. Mother had prepared all our favorite dishes, and next to Grandma, she was the best cook in the world. But the day dragged. We could hardly wait until it was time to go to Grandma's.

At last 3:30 came. Bundled up to our ears and laden with gifts, my family and Aunt May and Uncle Walt and their family, who lived on our street, trudged up to Ninth East to catch the streetcar. When we left the streetcar at Fourth East, my brother, cousins and I ran through the snow to see who could wish Grandma "Merry Christmas!" first.

Grandma was watching for us and threw wide the door, giving each a hug and a kiss and telling us to take off our wraps and get warm. The homey dining and kitchen room was warm and inviting as usual. The great rockers had been placed close to the huge coal range with its oven door open, ready to toast cold feet and hands. Oh, it was a pleasant place to be! We always felt loved and sheltered there.

When we were all present, Grandma opened the door into the parlor. There was the usual large Christmas tree with all of our favorite ornaments, colorful popcorn balls and small Christmas stockings. She hadn't forgotten to make our usual tree gifts, and she had waited until we arrived to light the candles. This was as it had always been. We solemnly watched my father as he put a match to each candle and "oohed" and "aahed" with each flicker. Uncle Walt stood on the other side of the tree to see that nothing caught fire.

The candles flickering in the dusk seemed to light the way into the unknown. To us, this was the climax of Christmas Day. Then, too soon, the candles were reluctantly blown out.

Then we gave our gifts to Grandma, and she gave a gift to each of us. It was a merry time, even though all of us there were aware of a missing face in the family circle.

We returned to the cozy dining room and kitchen. With our help and hindrance, along with much laughter and teasing, Grandma fixed cocoa, sandwiches, fruitcake, candy and nuts. We all gathered around the family table just like other Christmases.

The time flew and finally Uncle Walt looked at his Ingersol watch and said it was time to go. By making many trips to the outside toilet and eating slowly, we delayed our departure for a while. Eventually, though, we were all ready.

When we reached the car stop, we realized it had snowed some more during our visit. The tracks were covered with snow. We waited and waited. After half an hour, my father sent us back to the house to keep warm. We were to watch, and when he whistled, we were to run for it. But another half-hour passed—and still no car.

Finally, after waiting awhile longer, they decided that the tracks had too much snow on them and the cars couldn't run. We were snowbound at Grandma's.

Nothing like this had ever happened before. We were to stay all night at Grandma's—and on Christmas night, too!

That was a night to remember. Grandma found us assorted nightwear, and when we were ready, we gathered around her rocking chair close by the open oven and she read from the Bible the story of the first Christmas. The firelight flickered as heads began to nod. We all sweetly sang *Silent Night*, then my father said a prayer thanking God for His Gift to us and for our safe place to rest. Soon we were asleep, safe and secure at Grandma's house.

The next morning was one never to be forgotten, as we all surrounded the big table for breakfast. The blessing spoken over the food also thanked God for our safekeeping, our family unity and all our many blessings. Grandma and Mother cooked pancakes as only they could, along with cereal, eggs and milk.

By noon the streetcars were running again and we went home, fully aware that we had experienced a really choice Christmas. Little did we realize that it was the last Christmas we would spend in the adobe house on Fourth East. ✷

My First Sleigh Ride by John Slobodnik, House of White Birches nostalgia archives

Christmas of Yore

By Rose Hawkins

There is so much straw in that bob-sled and we are all bundled up. Then Grandpa says, "Giddy-up!" We start with a jerk and everyone hollers.

It is fun riding in that sled, but soon Grandma says, "Slow down! Here is our first stop—the Browns." Grandpa carefully handles a basket of goodies, for the Browns have six children.

A big candle shining in the window lights our way to the door. We knock, and as the door opens, we hear music, a guitar and singing— *The First Noel*. We stop and listen to another song—*Oh Little Town of Bethlehem*. Everyone is happy, singing and clapping their hands.

We stay awhile before Grandma insists we start on, as she has more people to see. Back into that straw! What fun! Soon, through some trees, down a lane, a light shines. Grandpa stops. Another basket is lifted out. This is the home of their friends Antonio and his wife. They are old people—older than Grandpa and Grandma.

Grandpa opens the door and says, "It is I, your neighbor," for Antonio is crippled and is seated with his accordion on his lap. Near the fireplace is a manger with a doll for the Baby Jesus, and all about are carved wooden animals with shepherds and wise men. Antonio asks us to join him in singing *Joy to the World* and *Away in the Manger*.

After exchanging holiday good wishes and shaking hands, we depart for one more stop, down the road apiece. By now there is frost around the mouths of the horses, so they keep shaking their heads and their bells really ring. I am beginning to fall asleep so Grandpa gets some snow and washes my face. That really wakes me!

We stop at a white house. Here, Grandma carries one of her bundles—a new quilt—and Grandpa brings a large box of goodies. These are newcomers to the neighborhood and Grandma says they must be welcomed and not be lonely during the Christmas season.

Nearing the door, we hear a Victrola playing *We Three Kings*. "Good singing," says Grandpa. After we give them our greetings, we all sing *O Come All Ye Faithful* and *It Came Upon a Midnight Clear*.

Again, Grandma insists that we must go, as it is getting late. "Our young one must be abed," she says. The straw in the bobsled is cold now, and I am so sleepy, so Grandpa sings *Jingle Bells* to the accompaniment of our own "jingle bells" on the harness.

Home at last! But Grandma says, "Sit a spell." I know what she is going to do, but I pretend it is a surprise. She starts singing *Silent Night* and Grandpa and I join in. Then she says, "I will tell you the story of a visit from heaven."

I listen. It is a beautiful story, but I fall asleep and have to be carried to bed. The next morning, as we ride to church in the sleigh, Grandma explains Christmas to me.

From her I really learn the value of sharing and happiness. I cuddle up close to her and say, "This is the nicest, bestest Christmas ever!" ❄

> *It is fun riding in that sled, but soon Grandma says, "Slow down! Here is our first stop—the Browns." Grandpa carefully handles a basket of goodies, for the Browns have six children.*

Christmas at Granny's

By Frances Grimes Yeargin

At Grandmother Johnson's house, every Christmas was a big event, and it is Christmas there that I remember best— like how Granny's little white house looked on Christmas Eve. There was always a lighted tree in the widest window, and as we stepped up onto the porch we could see "a good fire" crackling in the fireplace. As we entered, cousins, aunts and uncles swarmed around us. In the midst of it all was frail, spry, little Grandmother, happy to have her children together again for one more Christmas.

We unpacked our bags and tried to sneak our gifts under the tree. Someone remembered a forgotten item, so off we went in "The Bug" (Aunt Bess' faithful little 1932 Ford coupe) to make a last, frantic search through the crowded small-town business district.

We returned—and then someone remembered that we hadn't yet bought fruit for the stockings. This last phrase was whispered if any young grandchildren were around. Off we went in The Bug again to pick out the biggest, reddest apples and the largest, brightest oranges.

At last we completed preparations, except for hanging the stockings, which youngsters had been hanging on Granny's mantel since 1889. Years earlier we had given up hanging our own stockings in favor of Aunt Bess' long ones, which stretched and held more presents. Aunt Bess obligingly saved clean, old, silk stockings shot with runs, and we hung them on the mantel with a name tag pinned to each toe. A jar of Granny's plum jelly and a spoon were left nearby so Santy could have a special treat.

With this ceremony over, the house settled down to comparative quiet. If the night was clear, Granny would step out into the back yard and say to one of her grandchildren, "See? That's the Christmas star! It always shines brighter on Christmas Eve than any other night. I've seen it every Christmas for years."

I liked to stay up late on Christmas Eve, though I was always warned that Santy would "throw stuff in my eyes" if I didn't hurry to bed. But I liked to listen to the beautiful Christmas music on the radio and hear Big Ben chime as Christmas Day began in London. I usually helped Aunt Bess finish wrapping her presents. She was always the last to finish because she had been so busy doing so much for everyone else's Christmas.

Christmas Day at Grandmother's began with someone shouting, "Christmus gif!" Soon everyone was wide awake and shouting, too, trying to be the first to "get" the others with this old-fashioned greeting.

We ran in to see our bulging stockings hanging from the mantel. The children found toys in their stockings, but the grown-ups had only fruit, nuts and big peppermint sticks with a sassy note signed by Santy. We noticed a big spoonful of jelly was gone from the jar.

After emptying our stockings, we got back into bed to peel and eat our oranges. This gave the house time to get warm. Then we got up again, dressed and went to the kitchen where Granny had the turkey baking and the coffee perking. Granny always kept plenty of good, hot coffee on hand. She only used Maxwell House—until Edgar Bergen and his puppet started advertising Chase & Sanborn. She liked that program. She would ask, "Are you ready for some Charlie?" as she offered a cup of coffee.

Uncle Hayne and I were always ready for coffee. Uncle Hayne sipped his and commented, "This coffee is so strong, Mama, I'm afraid it'll make hair grow on the bottom of my feet!" But he drank it appreciatively.

Finally everyone was "ready to have the tree." The tree was always cedar, until Cousin Fran developed an allergy. After that it was a spruce or an East Texas pine.

When we were younger and taking music and expression and dancing lessons, we used to put on a program before the tree. My number was always a piano solo, a fancy arrangement of *Silent Night*.

Usually one of the grandsons was appointed to pass out the presents. One year, Minerva, then a little 10-year-old blonde, dressed up in a Santy costume. A slimmer, funnier Santy has never served our family!

After the tree had been stripped and everyone had admired everyone else's presents, the boys went out to shoot firecrackers. The women and girls went back to the kitchen to help with dinner. There was always fudge, patience, divinity and date loaf, and Granny always made fruitcake the weekend after Thanksgiving Day. She also made Osborn's favorite pineapple cake or Uncle Hayne's Minnehaha cake.

I remember best how Granny's little white house looked on Christmas Eve. There was always a lighted tree in the widest window, and as we stepped up onto the porch we could see "a good fire" crackling in the fireplace.

Granny always made the turkey and dressing, and giblet gravy. She always lectured about people who insisted on making dressing out of stale light bread. Granny used only freshly baked biscuits and corn bread. Aunt Lula always made the heavenly hash, a delicious dessert of whipped cream, maraschino cherries and marshmallows. The girls usually helped Aunt Bess make the salads and set the table, which was apt to be decorated with a toy Santa riding down the center in his sleigh, drawn by celluloid reindeer. My mother and the other aunts made the vegetables and other less interesting dishes.

Just about the time everybody had finished eating, Old Kate appeared. She was an ancient woman who had been my grandmother's maid when my mother was born. Old Kate continued to call Mother "my baby," which amused us. She referred to all of the family as "my white folks." Every year Old Kate came around for a Christmas visit and was warmly greeted and ushered into the kitchen. She seated herself comfortably and set her empty basket at her feet. Then she began to talk. Hearing her was worth anyone's while. She knew all the gossip of the town and told it in the most colorful and picturesque way. As she talked, she ate a heaping plate of food. And she always left with her basket well filled.

If the day was not rainy, Mother got out her Kodak for a round of taking pictures—"because next year we may not all be together." Then some of the older children had to leave; Osborn got only the day off from work, or Mert had to get back that night to "play for a dance." The kids went to the picture show. Others sat around and talked and listened to the radio. Late in the afternoon we had a snack of leftovers. As soon as night fell, we had a fireworks display of sparklers, rockets and Roman candles.

Christmas was over except for The Day After Christmas, when we always had a lunch of collards and corn bread. Uncle Hayne liked collards and could not buy them in West Texas. Anyway, this simple meal tasted good after the rich Christmas dinner.

And that is how we celebrated Christmas at my grandmother's house in the 1920s, 1930s and 1940s. ❄

© John Sloane

© John Sloane

A Swedish Christmas

By Gladys Hedstrom

Nothing, absolutely nothing, can dim the glory of my memories of childhood Christmases at Grandma's. (Why we called the farm "Grandma's" rather than "Grandpa's," I'll never know.)

Until I was 6 years old in 1910, our family of two boys, three girls and our parents lived in the fertile farmlands of Stark County in central Illinois, several miles from our grandparents' farm.

After our joyous Christmas morning at home, followed by breakfast, the seven of us climbed into a wagon on runners drawn by two bay horses. There were no sleigh bells, no carols. We didn't need any. The magical anticipation of another Christmas at Grandma's made us oblivious to the cold nipping at our nostrils. We rode past fields with snow drifted high against hedgerows. A few more miles and the hubbub of grandparents, uncles, aunts and cousins greeted us.

We children endured the delay as the adults sat in the central dining and living room, exchanging farm talk. Warming ourselves close to the heating stove, we were bursting to see the Christmas tree in the parlor.

Finally we saw it, a glorious fir strung with popcorn and cranberries. Glass icicles sparkled in the flickering light of red and white candles. The smell of wax droplets on fragrant evergreen branches is among my vivid memories of childhood Christmases.

First we admired the decorations. Then we pulled rocking chairs and straight-back chairs closer to enjoy the candlelight and wait for the fun to come.

Our usual interest in the rest of the parlor, opened only on Sundays and holidays, faded before the magic of the tree. On the marble-topped table under our grandparents' wedding pictures, the stereoscope and scenes of faraway places lay untouched. The croquinot-checkers table stayed folded behind the door. No one struggled to open the big golden clasp on the album covered with red velvet, bulging with family photographs. It occupied a place of importance next to the kerosene lamp whose double globes were painted with pink roses.

Then all the grand-children gathered in the dining room, where large plates were set for us at a side table. On each was a Swedish coffeecake surrounded by English walnuts and an orange (goodies seen only at Christmas), a cluster of raisins, ribbon and rock candy, peppermints, Brazil nuts, almonds and hazelnuts. Later each of us received a quarter, given to parents for safekeeping.

By today's standards, we should have been disappointed in our gifts. We weren't. Didn't *all* grandparents give coffeecake, candy and nuts instead of toys?

Dinner preparations had been going on intermittently, undertaken by Grandma and our aunts. Fascinated by the activities in the sunny kitchen, those of us who got in the way were given little chores, like getting more corncobs for the box by the range or pumping water at the sink for the hot-water tank on one side of the stove.

Some of us were sure to follow Aunt Minnie down into the cold cellar, where the dank odor of the earthen floor mingled with the mealy smell of potatoes and apples. From the shelves of preserved fruit and vegetables, she would select whatever was needed for the table set the full length of the dining room.

Goose or chicken was usually the main dish. If the latter, we children had the fun of pulling wishbones, with the advantage always in our favor. Mashed potatoes and gravy, and an array of vegetables were followed by my favorite, the dessert. The only trouble was in choice—mince or pumpkin pie or yellow cake with chocolate frosting. If I remember my grandmother correctly, she probably urged us to have some of each. Being Swedish, the adults had coffee, though my grandfather preferred cold tea. We children drank milk from tall, opalescent blue glasses.

After our joyous Christmas morning at home, followed by breakfast, the seven of us climbed into a wagon on runners drawn by two bay horses.

To keep us out from underfoot during dishwashing time, we were sent to the parlor to play games. Later the adults joined us in croquinot, checkers, "Who Am I?" and other games. The Christmas tree cast a soft radiance that made everything more fun. We didn't want the day to end.

At Grandma's insistence, we had supper after our late-afternoon games. Then, our sacks of goodies in hand, we made the round of goodbyes and were off into the frosty night. The cutting sound of metal runners on the snow and the clop-clopping of horses' hooves were barely heard above our chatter. Moonlight gleamed blue and cold across the fields. Once past our one-room schoolhouse and Owen's orchard, we were home.

After a short session with our gifts, still strewn in the living room, we children were ready for bed. Frost crystals etched an ever-widening border around the windowpanes as we quickly fell asleep, wrapped in the lingering warmth of another Christmas Day at Grandma's. ❄

Grandma's House for Christmas

By Afton Brown

I love to go to Grandma's
to spend the holiday;
To smell the goodies baking
And hear my Granddad say,

"I think I hear the sleigh bells
Of St. Nick upon the roof;
Now listen mighty closely
And you'll hear the reindeer hoof."

I'd strain my ears to listen;
"I hear them now, I know,"
The silvery *tinkle, tinkle* of
Phantom sleigh bells 'cross the snow.

No matter how we scurried
To dash out in the night,
The fleet feet of the reindeer
Had whisked him out of sight.

But Grandpa, he just chuckled,
His merry eyes aglow,
Gave each of us a mighty hug,
"Now off to bed you go."

So up the long, dark staircase
And down the narrow hall,
The coal-oil lamp a-flickerin'
Cast weird shadows on the wall.

We shivered in the chillness
Of the murky, dim-lit room,
Then leaped into the feather bed,
Hoping morning would come soon.

But would it ever really come?
It seemed so far away,
Must be at least a thousand years,
The longed-for Christmas day!

Finally slumber drew its draperies
O'er my heavy-laden eyes;
The millennium night passed quickly.
Behold! the wint'ry morning skies.

We scampered in our nightshirts
As swiftly as could be
Downstairs into the parlor …
Lo! The Christmas tree!

With candles all a-glowing,
Glistening tinsel—what a sight!—
There right upon the very top
A brilliant star shone bright!

'Neath the tree's sparkling splendor,
Were there for me some toys?
Oh, those holidays at Grandma's,
Wondrous Christmas joys!

Ere the morn was over,
Ere the noon would chime,
The folks all started coming …
'Twas almost dinnertime.

Aunts and uncles and young 'uns,
My! How things were buzzin'!
Nieces, nephews and kinfolk,
Cousins by the dozen!

We gathered 'round the plenteous board,
A feast fit for a king.
Grandfather, with humility,
Then thanked God for everything.

Oh, how I long to go once more
Down childhood paths to roam,
And spend another Christmas
At Grandma and Grandpa's home!

Over the River and Through the Woods

By Dorothy Jean Schroeder

When my two sisters and I were children, we had something very special, something that only our older brothers and a few cousins shared. We had our silver-haired grandmother, who lived in a picturesque log house that was nestled on a hill amongst tall evergreens. The house had a full-length porch where we could sit and look down into the green valley below. On clear days, Pilchuck Mountain was visible in the distance.

We were even luckier than our cousins because we lived on a small farm in that valley. We could see Grandma's log house from our home.

Whenever our mother said, "Let's go see Mama," we would quickly put our toys aside. We three sisters, Millie, June and I, loved to walk through the green pastures and up the trail to Grandma's house.

It was about a half-mile to the edge of the woods. After we entered the woods, it was a short walk to the base of a wide trail, which was shadowed by tall evergreens and padded with pine needles.

The trail wasn't very long, but it was quite steep, so steep that if I started running going back down, I couldn't stop until I reached the bottom—that is, unless I stumbled and fell. I know, because I fell more than once. That didn't cure me of running, but it taught me to be more surefooted.

Most of our aunts and uncles and cousins gathered at the log house several times a year for special occasions such as Grandma's birthday and Mother's Day. But Christmas was the most special day of all.

Living in the woods, Grandma had her choice of trees to decorate. When I was a child, her Christmas tree seemed very tall to me; it almost reached the ceiling. Old-fashioned decorations graced its branches: chains made of red and green paper, strings of sparkling tinsel, hand-painted ornamental balls, popcorn, small cellophane dolls and soldiers—and last but not least, candy canes.

How I remember the anticipation as we waited for the sound of heavy footsteps on the porch! If it was accompanied by the merry jingle of sleigh bells, we knew without a doubt that Santa had arrived.

Santa would enter the living room with a bag of toys slung over his back and call out a jolly "Ho, ho, ho!" Ours was a real storybook Santa, wearing a red suit and cap trimmed with white fur. He also had the classic long white beard, bushy white eyebrows and a well-rounded tummy. What a thrill it was for those innocents among us who still believed in Santa Claus and the Tooth Fairy to see him coming through that door!

Holiday Sleigh Ride by Sam Timm, courtesy of Wild Wings Inc. on pages 128 and 129

Some of my aunts greeted Santa as if he were an old friend, asking about his trip from the North Pole—that sort of thing. And I still remember how my Aunt Daisy giggled at the time.

But Santa was a busy man so he didn't have time to dally. He put his pack on the floor, reached in for a gift, then called out a name. There was a gift for each of my cousins, my sisters, my brothers and me—all of the children. I can't recall what the others got, but I usually got a book because Santa seemed to know what I wanted most.

Most of our aunts and uncles and cousins gathered at the log house several times a year for special occasions. But Christmas was the most special day of all.

Then, one Christmas, the unthinkable happened. One of my cousins discovered that Santa Claus was a phony, that the man in the red Santa suit was actually a favorite uncle. And when the innocents argued, the guilty one said she could prove it! She showed us where we could peek into Grandma's bedroom in the corner where the curve of the logs met the straight edge of the wall.

What child could resist such a challenge? We girl cousins each took a peek and, sure enough, there he was—stuffing pillows into the red Santa suit!

We will never know how the secret of our lost innocence was leaked to those who chose to preserve the fable of Santa Claus. I only know that the following Christmas, all of us children had to wait together in a small, vacant house a short distance from Grandma's house. We had to wait there until just before Santa made his grand entrance.

There were a few more Christmas celebrations on the hill before Grandma left her beloved log house and moved down into the valley. Sadly, when she was about 70, walking up the hill to her cabin after going "downtown" to Machias became too difficult for her.

We never realized then how much we were blessed; we enjoyed a storybook Christmas in a storybook log house. Although it has been more than 50 years since we gathered at Grandma's house for the last time, I still remember the happy days of long ago, and I will always cherish those memories. ✳

One Christmas the unthinkable happened. One of my cousins discovered that Santa Claus was a phony …

When We Went to Grandfather's

By H.W.B.

"We are going to Grandfather's for Christmas!"

How excited we all were as Ned dashed into the room waving the letter above his head. We had spent several summers on the farm in Connecticut, but had never been there in the winter.

We started on Christmas Eve. I was wild with excitement and couldn't understand how Father could read his paper so calmly on the train, while Mother and Annette talked of commonplace things and the boys looked out the window as if it were an ordinary journey.

As we left the train, the sun was setting, filling the waters of Long Island Sound with a golden radiance and casting long blue shadows on the snow. I have never known it to be so cold. Our breath came in clouds of steam from our lips, and the air was full of tiny, icy particles that stung our cheeks until they glowed scarlet. We were glad to snuggle down into the buffalo robes in the waiting sleigh.

As the stars came out I looked up at a big one in the East and pretended we were following it to the Christ Child, like the Wise Men. I was so occupied with my dream that we reached Warren almost before I knew it.

Grandmother brought us into the living room, before the huge fireplace that burned whole logs. Great-grandmother's hooks and trammels still hung in it, and at one side was the Dutch oven she used to heat with hot coals and bake bread and pies in.

While we were at supper, Hiram had brought in armfuls of evergreen, and while Bob and I popped corn, Ned and Annette decorated the hall and rooms, finally driving us away from our nooks so that festoons could be hung from the mantel. Then each brought his stocking, and when they were hung along the edge, slim and hungry-looking, we knew it was really, truly Christmas Eve!

After Mother had kissed me goodnight it took me a long time to get to sleep. The room was filled with queer little winter wood-creaks, and I could hear the bare branches scrape against my window. And I kept wondering if there would be club skates in my stocking in the morning. I wanted them more than anything else in the world.

I was awake and dressed before daylight, and Bob and I went creeping down the shut-in back staircase, with its queer, old-house smell. A fire burned brightly in the living-room fireplace—our stockings had been carefully hung to one side— and we were soon deep in the midst of our presents. A little shiver of joy went over me when I found the club skates. Then, all of a sudden, from the upper hallway came floating, "Hark! The herald angels sing!" Annette and Ned were waking the family.

We had a jolly breakfast, though little was eaten, everyone being so busy untying parcels and thanking one another. Afterward we children went down to skate.

The pond was covered with new ice, so clear that you could look through to the dark, mysterious water. Our Christmas skates took us over the frozen surface like birds, but it was too cold to stay very long. When we got back to the house our noses and ears were numb, and oh, how they stung as we thawed out before the fire!

Bob and I played with my new farmyard until dinnertime, but it was hard to think about anything with those heavenly whiffs of turkey

John Clymer

and plum pudding coming from the region of the kitchen. There never was such a dinner in all the world!

Afterward, Mother and the aunts played all our new games with us while Father and Grandmother talked in the flickering light of the fire. Then, when I was too sleepy to keep my eyes open, Father carried me up to bed, and after I was undressed, Mother came in for the goodnight kiss.

"It's been the happiest Christmas I ever had," I said as she tucked me in, "but I wish we had followed the star to the Christ Child."

"We have, Sweetheart," replied Mother softly. "We find the Christ Child every Christmas in all the simple joy and love that comes then."

"Oh!" I murmured, and fell asleep. ❋

Christmas Day at Grandpa Gray's

By Mrs. Wesley Gray

Christmas Day at Grandpa Gray's
Was surely an event.
All the relatives gathered there each year;
We knew just what it meant.

But first, a rush for stockings
To view the contents o'er.
We knew they would be filled to the top;
Santa always came before.

Mom called us all to breakfast;
We had no appetite.
We tried to eat a little
Just to show we were polite.

The chores all done, Dad went to hitch
The horses to the sleigh.
We all piled in with nice, warm robes;
Dad had put in some hay.

The air was crisp; the miles soon sped
And we were at the door,
Grandma standing there to welcome us
As she had done so many times before.

The guests were all assembled,
All in their Sunday best,
And Grandma and Grandpa
Were as happy as the rest.

The table in the dining room
Was loaded with good eats …
The turkey with all its trimmings,
Mince pie, and all those treats.

So many volunteered to help
To wash and clear away
The remains of the dinner
On this glad Christmas Day.

We went into the parlor.
Grandma played the organ as we sang
Those good old Christmas hymns;
The air with music rang.

And as the sun was sinking low,
Time to go home had come,
But not before we sang together
That dear old *Home Sweet Home*.

Grandpa Gray has left us,
But memories linger still;
And we remember those happy times
On Christmas at Rose Hill.

1938 *Farmer's Wife*, House of White Birches nostalgia archives

The Red Mittens

By Faye Underwood

There seems to be a time in childhood when all the senses are enhanced and finely attuned. Everything appears vivid and larger than life. My 10th year was that magical year for me.

The world and everything in it seemed wondrous. As the holidays approached, my elation mounted until it became one big, swirling bubble of anticipation. Even the sight of the mailman coming down the snow-banked road set my heart fluttering. There just might be a package hanging from the mailbox!

The only thing marring its perfection was the fact that Grandmother would not be with us to share Christmas. She had passed away in September, as quietly as the leaves sifting from the maple. Her gifts to us had always been practical, handmade items, things for our personal comfort—warm socks for Dad, a bright muffler for Mother, caps or mittens for us kids. They were essentials during the bitter Wisconsin winter, when we braved deep snowdrifts on the way to school.

Grandmother never "held" with store-bought goods. "Just won't hold up," she would say with a disdainful shrug. And so she kept busily knitting away, putting her stamp of craftsmanship and love in every stitch.

In her later years, after all her family had left home, I would spend the night with her. After supper, when twilight fell, she would light the old oil lamp, sit in her rocking chair and pick up her basket of yarn. I can still see her, the clicking needles setting a tempo as she rocked. With a twinkle in her blue eyes, she would ask, "And what color this year—maybe green?" It was our own private little joke, because she knew my favorite color was red.

That year my two older brothers had outdone themselves. They had scouted the woods beyond the pasture until they found the tallest, bushiest white pine of them all. It stood ready on the back porch. It was our family tradition for Mother and Dad to set up and trim the tree after we kids had gone to bed on Christmas Eve. They wanted us to have the thrill of seeing it for the first time Christmas morning.

The last few days preceding Christmas dragged slowly, but at last Christmas Eve arrived. The lamp shed a soft glow as we sat around the table stringing popcorn and cranberry ropes.

Mother had the old wood-burning range going full blast in the kitchen, and the aroma of bubbling mincemeat mingled with the spiciness of baking cookies. Later we had our treats of milk and cookies, then sang carols before mounting the stairs to bed.

At the first light of dawn we were awake for the big day. Whispering in glee, we congregated at the head of the stairs, waiting for the sounds of stirring below. Then in unison we called, "Can we come down now, Dad?"

"Just a minute," he answered with a chuckle. He had just enough time to light the candles on the tree and put out the goodies!

At his signal, we rushed down the stairs. We were always overwhelmed by our first glimpse of the tree. There it stood in regal splendor, its pine scent permeating the room. The candles in tiny tin holders, lit now to enjoy for a few brief moments, reflected and shimmered on the tinsel ropes.

In one mad scramble we found our presents. Paper flew in all directions in our haste to discover the treasures within.

After all the packages had been opened, there came a lull in activity, and I saw Mother and Dad exchange meaningful looks. Mother arose, went into the bedroom and returned carrying packages wrapped in plain brown paper and tied with bits of yarn. "I was asked to give you these," she said solemnly. A shadow fell over her face as she handed them out. We all knew who the donor was.

The room became very still, and in that moment, I'm sure we all felt Grandmother's presence. I couldn't bring myself to look up at my parents, but sat with bowed head, stroking the soft wool of my red mittens.

How typical of Grandmother! Methodically she had put her house in order in those last few months, even to remembering our handmade gifts—her gifts of love. ✳

1928 *Home Arts Needlecrafts*, House of White Birches nostalgia archives

ALICE BEACH WINTER

A Christmas Memory

By David A. Conner

Grandma, as she loved to be called, was the mother of five children and the grandmother of 13. She was constantly doing things for her family and friends, and was always there for those who needed a helping hand or wise counsel. Grandma had an understanding heart and held a generous regard for everyone around her. She tried to always think good of others. To her, Christmas was special.

The Christmas tree came from the woods in back of my grandparents' farmhouse. Every year Grandma would go into the woods to get it. She would chop the tree down, drag it to the house, stand it in the "back room" and trim it all by herself so that it would be ready for the big day.

No one was without a gift, as Grandma had one for every person. Either it was something she had made or something she had bought especially for the recipient.

On Christmas Eve, as was the family custom, everyone went to her home. It was a full house, as all of my relatives and some of my grandparents' friends had come to take Christmas Eve dinner and share in the opening of the gifts afterward.

I will always remember my grandmother standing by her old wood-burning cookstove, stirring something, then turning to us to say hello as we entered the house. Then she'd ask how we were doing and what we wanted Santa to bring us that night.

When Grandma had finished cooking and the evening meal had finally found its way onto the old, round oak table, everyone would gather

I will always remember my grandmother standing by her old wood-burning cookstove, stirring something, then turning to us to say hello as we entered the house.

in or around the small kitchen, and a prayer would be said. After the prayer, the grown people would eat first, during which some last-minute present wrapping would be going on in the back room. As the last of the children finished eating and when everyone had finally arrived, all conversation and other activities stopped, and we all moved into the back room, anticipating all the gifts that were spread out under the tree.

Once everyone was settled, we would stand to sing a few Christmas carols, one of which was always *Silent Night*, my grandmother's favorite. Then began the opening of the presents, which were handed out by some of the younger grandchildren. All had a gleam in their eyes as they received their gifts. The room was filled with joy, laughter and excitement as we opened them. After thanking everyone and looking at all of the opened presents, there were cakes, fruit and nuts to eat before the evening came to an end.

After those who weren't staying for the night had left, the rest of us would pick out the places where we wanted to sleep. All the rooms of that small farmhouse were filled. I would sometimes get to sleep in the living room, listening to the peaceful chiming of the mantel clock in the cold, dark silence that shrouded the house inside and out. Lying there, I felt peaceful and happy.

Those days and times are long since gone and my grandmother has been gone for some years. But what hasn't left are the precious memories. They will always be mine. ❄

We're Home by Charles Berger, House of White Birches nostalgia archives

If Only in My Dreams

Chapter Six

"I'll be home for Christmas." So went the song and so went the hopes and dreams of many young American men and women through the four long years of World War II. Like every war before and after, we dreamed of young men, attired in the dress uniforms of each branch of service, gathered in laughter and gaity for a good dose of holiday cheer.

But that was not reality for families back then, and all too often since. These stories are dedicated to the millions of fighting men and women who have sacrificed their season of peace for the security of our nation.

In the 1940s, from the European theater of war to the South Pacific, from defense plants to the family farm—no family went without knowing of sacrifice for world security.

And, while we all gave willingly to the cause, we also knew the profound loss. Many lost fathers, sons, husbands, uncles, cousins and friends. Those who didn't at least lost time. Years for children to be without fathers. Months waiting for furloughs. Weeks waiting for word from loved ones. Days that seemed like decades. No time of the year was it more apparent than at Christmas.

"I'll be home for Christmas."

It was a promise that largely went unfulfilled for most of us. While the war raged on, we found the true meaning of melancholy. Even when we knew for a certainty that our loved ones were safe—and we rarely knew that—their absence at the yuletide season made each wartime Christmas that much harder to bear.

How many mothers ached for word from sons? How many sweethearts and wives looked for a special V-Mail note? And how many times did we wish for the war to cease, especially around the season of peace?

"I'll be home for Christmas"—and we knew it was ultimately true. Because those who spent Christmas on the front were kept close to the hearts of those who spent Christmas on the home front. Though thousands of miles apart, separated by oceans and continents, the prayers of every family gathered around a holiday table were directed toward all of the empty chairs in kitchens and dining rooms around the nation.

And we all knew the meaning of the words of that favorite song: "I'll be home for Christmas—if only in my dreams."

—*Ken Tate*

An Unforgettable Card

By Frances M. Callahan

On Dec. 24, 1943, I received a Christmas card I will never forget. Two generations have been added to our family in the intervening years; yet, each year, when Christmas cards start coming, time seems to telescope like an old-fashioned collapsible drinking cup, and vivid memories of that long-ago holiday season flood my mind.

Christmas cards started arriving in mid-December of 1943. Each day as I returned home from my job at an aircraft factory, the mail was uppermost in my mind. Anxiously I would riffle through the envelopes hoping to find one bearing a Fleet P.O. return address. At their respective homes, my parents and two sisters were all keeping equally close tabs on their mailboxes, for it had been more than two months since any of us had heard from my only brother.

If any of us were to find that long-hoped-for and prayed-for envelope in our mail, we didn't really expect it would hold a Christmas card. All we wanted, with all our hearts, was a short note of any kind, or a V-mail letter scrawled in Bud's inimitable hand.

True, there had been other long periods without word from him since he, along with thousands of other Marines, had stormed the beaches at Guadalcanal on Aug. 7, 1942. But the thought of not knowing where he was—or how he was—at Christmastime seemed nearly unbearable.

Yet day after long December day went by without that envelope arriving. As the family's anxiety grew, we tried to be supportive of each other, repeating the old cliché: "No news is good news." But of course, that much-overworked saying was of small consolation in view of the war news coming from the South Pacific in those dreadful days.

By the 22nd of December the influx of holiday mail had dwindled to a mere trickle. On the 23rd only one greeting card arrived, and it was not the right one. My heart sank; my hopes vanished. Christmas just wouldn't be Christmas this year. Bud was a career Marine in his ninth year of service, and this would be the first Christmas there had been no card or holiday letter from him. We are a family with strong ties; we keep in touch. Were we now another family destined to be ravaged by the war? I slept very little that night, and went to work the next day with a heavy heart.

On my return from work I found the mailbox filled with envelopes. Apparently the post office's campaign to "Mail early!" had been ignored by quite a few of my friends! After taking off my coat, I picked up the sheaf of letters I had laid on the table when I came into the house.

Then, there it was—the third envelope down in the stack. I would have recognized the handwriting among a hundred others!

Breathing a quick, prayerful sigh of relief, my anxious fingers quickly tore open the long-awaited envelope. Pulling out the card, I barely noticed the picture on the front; I was searching for the personal note I knew I would find on the card or on an enclosed piece of paper.

Opening the card, I found my brother's short but welcome note on the left portion of the center crease. It was dated Dec. 12 and as I read the words, I was still very aware that during war, battles are fought and men die in much less time than had elapsed since he had written the card.

My eyes brimmed with tears as I finished reading Bud's note. I breathed a silent prayer of thanks for his well-being, and I beseeched God for his continued safety.

But he had been well when the brief note was written, and he had said, "Can't tell you where I am," which seemed to imply that he was no longer in Guadalcanal. We would learn months later that his company had indeed been moved to another island in the South Pacific.

My eyes brimmed with tears as I finished reading Bud's note. I breathed a silent prayer of thanks for his well-being, and I beseeched God for his continued safety, and to bring a swift end to the horrible war with its costly sacrifice of mankind. My heart filled with compassion for all the war-bereaved who would never again receive a letter or a Christmas card from loved ones who had made the supreme sacrifice. Encompassed in these agonizing thoughts, I wept uncontrollably and unashamedly for a long time.

Finally, when the flood of tears had passed, I picked up the card again and really saw it for the first time. On the half opposite my brother's note was a replica of a sleeve patch of the 1st Marine Division, Guadalcanal: a blue diamond with a large red numeral one standing vertically from the top to bottom points of the diamond. Small white letters reading "Guadalcanal" were in a perpendicular line in the large numeral. Printed in black and superimposed over the patch design were the words, "Peace on earth, good will toward men."

After reading these words, words as old as Christmas itself, I turned to the picture of the Marine patrol on the front of the card. It seemed an enigmatic combination: a scene of war with a message of peace. For a brief moment, I felt that it was sacrilegious.

Then, studying the picture, I raised my eyes from the figure of the Marine patrolling through the jungle night to the Christmas star. I suddenly thought, *Where could there be a greater and more sincere wish for "peace on earth and good will toward men" than in the hearts of military men from a peace-loving nation like our own? Who is better qualified to know the true blessings of peace than those who are suffering the horrors of war?*

In the many Christmas seasons that have come and gone since 1943, I have never received a more unforgettable Christmas card. To me, the picture on it is as soul-stirring as the

famous news photo of the flag-raising on Iwo Jima. I have often wished that the picture on that 1943 Marine Christmas card could have reached a larger audience—that it hadn't been confined to families and friends of the 1st Marine Division.

Several years after the close of World War II, I decided to preserve the picture from my card by having it framed. It was then that I noted, in very fine print on the back of the card, the credit notation of the design to a technical sergeant of the Marine Corps.

I began wondering about this man whose creative work had moved me so eloquently. Had he, like my brother, been one of the fortunate Marines to come back? What had been his feeling and emotions when he designed the card? If he had returned, would it be possible to locate him to ask these questions?

Through the cooperation of the historical branch of the U.S. Marine Corps in Washington, D.C., I was able to reach the former technical sergeant artist. In a gracious reply to my query, he wrote, "The idea I intended to show was the forces of peace-loving men tiredly moving out of the dark depth of a troubled, struggling world toward the inevitable peace symbolized by the age-old star of Bethlehem."

True, there has been no "World War" in the last five decades, but neither has there been worldwide peace. Will the pen (or man's words) never become mightier than the sword (or the bomb)?

As another yuletide approaches a still-turbulent world, surely there can be no more appropriate prayer in our hearts than the greeting inscribed on that Christmas card I received so many years ago. "Peace on earth, good will toward men." ❋

1917—Christmas in a Nation at War

By Terry D. Wright

My grandmother, Blanche Mae Dial Wright, sat in her big blue chair, diligently gazing at something in her hand. From my position in the doorway, I could not see what she was holding.

A white cardboard box, now yellowed and worn with age, lay in her lap. Bits of paper, ribbon and poems hastily cut from some long-forgotten newspaper protruded from the box.

The object in Grandma's hand was small, to be sure, and looked like an old political campaign button.

Startled by my entry, Grandma stopped turning the button over in her hand and looked up.

"Political button, Grandma?" I questioned.

"Oh, gracious no," she said. "Just a Christmas button from the Red Cross in 1917."

She handed me the 1½-inch machine-stamped lapel pin. I was surprised by the beautiful artwork on that dainty curio.

The button was gold and on the face was a nostalgic photo of Santa Claus. The detail in the old gent's face was exciting. He looked just like the kindly soul that children dreamed about each Christmas. Finally, there was a small red cross in the lower left corner and the date 1917 was stamped in black next to the red cross.

"Everyone wore those at Christmas in 1917," said Grandma as she looked up from the other memories overflowing the cardboard carton. "We wore them in remembrance of our boys in France who weren't having such a lovely time."

Grandma leaned back in comfort and closed her eyes for a moment as if being cast back in time.

Then she reminisced: "I wasn't married yet and many of the young people in our church group got together to make special Christmas packages for our boys overseas."

"Grandma," I asked, "Why do you always call them 'boys'?"

"Because that is what they were," she replied. "Boys. Many of them returned home after being gassed on the battlefields in Europe. Some were coming home without arms or legs. Oh, it was just awful.

"The pin reminded us all that we would not really enjoy Christmas until the soldiers were home.

"In the Red Cross and social clubs, young girls and even classes of school children would try to put kits together for the fighting men."

As a young girl growing up in Leavenworth, Kan., she had heard many tales of the war effort. Through church groups and civic organizations, Grandma became aware of the heroics of the common individual during the war. The wonderful women who were active in Europe certainly made an impression on Grandma. She heard stories of brave young women driving ambulances on the battlefields. She heard of nurses taking care of the wounded while they lived in dirt and dampness. The medical assistants had little hope of securing even a warm meal.

Grandma also told of women associated with the YWCA who were eager to go to the front lines and help. "The Allies were in need of typists, and many young women learned to type just for a chance to serve," she said. There were even other cases of women associated with the YWCA making doughnuts on the firing line!

Grandma admired both the spirit and endurance modeled by these individuals. "Those women," she said, "were not only admired by the soldiers but by all of us civilians back home who heard about their work.

"When we heard about such gallant individuals, we worked that much harder," said Grandma with a smile. "We spent hours rolling bandages or collecting dry socks and underwear for those weary men."

Grandma put her chin in her hand and appeared pensive. "The soldiers weren't the nly ones we prepared packages for, either. here were thousands of refugees from the war. Many Europeans had lost their homes and belongings. So we made Christmas boxes for hem and many others suffering in Europe.

"Christmas in 1917 was not the usual happy holiday for us here at home. We lived with the constant thought of those suffering in Europe.

"I'll tell you one thing," she said, wagging an emphatic finger toward me. "There were many people here who couldn't enjoy their Christmas dinner because of the thought of hose poor soldiers and refugees."

Grandma is gone now, but as I look hrough that box of memories today, I can find other traces of the war years. A crumbled, yellow-stained poem from a newspaper tells about some patriotic soldier dying on a foreign shore. An American flag neatly folded into a type of bunting. A small, round, glass frame with a young soldier's portrait, softly faded with age.

These were the lasting Christmas memories of a young girl and a nation at war. ❄

One Italian Christmas

By Gene Brewington

On Christmas Eve during the war, we were in some nameless village in the Apennine Mountains of Italy. We had seen a hundred villages just like it as we had fought, clawed and died on our way up the Italian peninsula.

We had been trying to take this village for three days. After days of shelling by the artillery and bombing by the "fly-boys," we finally had gained control. There were not three untouched houses remaining. The rest were complete or partial piles of rubble.

We moved into the village just before dusk. Outposts were placed, and perimeter guards were posted. An occasional incoming artillery shell was the only sign of the enemy. We were all dead on our feet. No hot meals for three days. No bath for a week.

Being a non-com, I was volunteered as sergeant of the guard. It was about 3 a.m., and I was checking my guard posts. Needless to say, I was down in the dumps; it was Christmas Eve, my third away from my family. Tonight there was no tree, no presents and probably not even a Santa Claus. Thousands of miles from home. Bitterly cold. No one cared whether I lived or died—not even me.

As I picked my way through, over and around the rubble, I was constantly alert. The soldier who survives in battle develops a sixth sense. As I passed a large pile of rubble that had once been a house, I thought I heard a moan. *It couldn't be. Nothing could be alive in that pile of trash.* Listening more closely, I heard it again. With my tommy gun ready, I listened more carefully. I finally ascertained from whence the noise came.

As I carefully moved rocks and pieces of timber, the crying became more distinct. I could not use a light, but with help from a sliver of moonlight, I finally saw a small, crumpled body beneath the rubble. After a few minutes of silent work, I reached in and pulled out a little Italian girl, perhaps 3 or 4 years old. She was hysterical, but although she was covered with dirt, she appeared to be in fair shape.

I picked her up and headed for the medics who were in one of the few still-standing buildings. Easing through the temporary blackout curtains, I deposited her on an examining table. I told one of the medics to clean her up and see if she had anything broken, and that I would be back later.

I returned about an hour later. They had washed her up and combed her hair. Miraculously, she had suffered only a few abrasions—nothing serious. They had given her water and food, and she was calmer.

She did not protest when I picked her up and wrapped her in my overcoat. My platoon had taken over a partially damaged mill house. Feeling my way through the darkness, I located my sleeping bag and crawled in, boots and all. I cuddled the little girl in my arms and zipped up the bag. She was soon fast asleep.

The grapevine works fast in the Army. It was not long after daylight when a runner shook me awake. "Report to the Old Man immediately."

The "Old Man" must have been at least 30 years old. Leaving the waif in the care of another soldier, I reported to the C.O. His first words were, "Sergeant, I hear you have been fraternizing with the enemy, and had a female in your sleeping bag last night. Yes or no?"

I explained as best I could.

"Dang it, Sergeant, you know we can't have civilians in camp with us," he replied. "You will have to get rid of her."

"Yes, Sir. I will get rid of her, at once—Sir. Shall I shoot her—Sir?"

"Don't be sarcastic, Sergeant. You can keep her today, but tomorrow you can take my jeep and driver, and take her to that convent we passed about 20 miles back."

"Yes, Sir," I replied, grinning to myself.

He dismissed me, but as I started for the door, he halted me. "Just a minute, Sarge." Digging through his duffel bag, he came up with a stuffed teddy bear. Looking back, it was laughable that an "old man" would carry a teddy bear. It looked brand-new. He said that he had been saving it to give to his daughter when he got home. As he handed me the toy, did I see a tear in the old so-and-so's eye? It

As I carefully moved rocks and pieces of timber, the crying became more distinct. I could not use a light, but with help from a sliver of moonlight, I finally saw a small, crumpled body beneath the rubble.

couldn't be. He was tough as a boot and twice as tall.

When I got back to my sleeping bag, she was awake and being entertained by half the company. There were always a few soldiers around who could speak Italian. They had learned her name was Lisa. Her parents were somewhere in the rubble. *"Morte! Morte!"*

Every man in the company must have visited Lisa that day. The company tailor, who doubled as a 74mm gunner, had whipped her up a dress and jacket. He had even made her underclothes, GI in color.

I will never know where they came from, but all kinds of toys appeared—even a doll that could say, "Ma-ma." She was given candy and fruit. All from a dirty, stinking, unkempt bunch of dogfaces, any one of whom could—and would—kill without blinking an eye. More love was given and received that Christmas Day so long ago than I have ever seen before or since.

As the jeep pulled away the next morning, Lisa, in her new GI uniform, cuddled in my lap as two duffel bags of goodies in back jostled over the rough roads. I thought of the gifts of the Magi so long ago. Maybe there is a spark of love in the world, in spite of man's inhumanity to man. Maybe there really *is* a Santa Claus. ❋

Christmas at the Pearl

By Eloise V. Wilson

When my children asked me recently what had been my favorite Christmas of all, it took me about a minute to answer. There never was a Christmas like the one we had in Honolulu, Hawaii, in 1941. We had been bombed a few weeks earlier; we were suffering the agonies of wondering when the Japanese would return; we had no idea where the Army had taken my brother; we were caught up in the unfamiliar duties of building bomb shelters and trying to stock them when food was rationed. There really was not a great deal to be joyous about that year, and yet, it was my favorite Christmas of all!

You would think that people living in the Hawaiian Islands might have had some inkling that war was imminent, and it's true that there were rumors from time to time, but there was little that people could do in those days to rattle our politicians, to force action from our president in the White House. We placed our trust in Franklin Delano Roosevelt and tried to ignore the warnings that surfaced periodically. We went along as though there would always be another tomorrow.

There were no Christmas parties, luaus or other festivities being planned—no rehearsals of Christmas concerts, pageants and carols to keep us busy. Instead we were busy digging bomb shelters.

As far back as 1931, there had been rumors. My father, owner of a baseball team, had taken the team to the Orient that year. When he returned home, he told my mother an unusual tale of having had his film confiscated because he had taken pictures of a steel factory. His guide had told him that Japan was preparing for a great war, and nobody was allowed to take pictures of their factories. "A great war"—surely he meant with China. He *couldn't* mean with the United States!

And then, in 1938, when I was about 7 years old, neighbors of ours sold their home, packed all their belongings and moved back to Japan. The children in the family didn't want to move to a land they had never known; Hawaii was their home. But their parents told them that Japan would someday rule the world, and they would be proud to be living in a land that was so powerful.

It was a lovely, sunny day, that seventh day of December in 1941. Nobody could have guessed the horror that would soon be on us. We liked to attend an early Mass on Sundays so that we could have more time for our special family day. My parents sat with four of us children in the church.

I think I was the first one to hear the bombs. Wanting to know what it was all about, I whispered to my father that I felt faint, and went outside for a drink of water. I quickly crossed the street to Waikiki Beach and stood in the sand, happily watching the airplanes in the sky. Off in the distance toward Pearl Harbor, I could see clouds of billowing black smoke. How authentic the war maneuvers seemed! I was fascinated!

My father found me there and frantically pushed me into the car as he explained that our parish priest had

Explosions rock Pearl Harbor (above) while two battleships (facing page) become an inferno on "the day of infamy."

announced we were being attacked by the Japanese. When we reached home, we rushed to turn on the radio while my father went out to search for my two older brothers who were delivering the morning newspaper.

Emory, my oldest brother, was in the National Guard, so he immediately reported to the armory. All that day we sat near the radio, listening, whispering, praying, wondering what was in store for us. Then an elderly, stooped, Japanese man came by on his daily rounds, carrying two buckets of sweetmeats for sale, hanging from his neck by a heavy pole. We didn't think it incongruous at all that we rushed out to buy treats from him. After all, we had many Japanese friends.

Schools were immediately closed, and that didn't displease us kids at all. The islands were placed under martial law, and we weren't quite sure what that would mean. People were asked to remain in their homes as much as possible, until the government could get some semblance of order back into our lives. We were ordered to obey a nightly curfew and to blacken our windows immediately so that there would be no lights visible at night.

I remember that first night and many nights afterward when neighbors from three families would gather at our house to spend the night. Ours was the largest house on the block, occupied by my grandparents, my parents, a spinster aunt, my four brothers, one sister and me. There really wasn't much room for houseguests, yet because it was the largest house on the block— or perhaps everyone thought there was safety in numbers—neighbors started to arrive every night right after dinner.

Gathered in the parlor, spilling over into the dining room, we'd huddle together and listen to the radio. During those many frightening nights, how great it was to listen to *Jack Benny, Allen's Alley, Red Skelton* and *Hit Parade*, just as if nothing had ever happened! I sometimes think it was the radio that kept us all going. After the newspapers had been read and put aside and the rumors tossed about and discussed, our radio became an authority and a friend.

That first night, we worried that the Japanese would return. It seemed impossible that they wouldn't. We were so unprepared for war; surely the islands would crumble immediately and we would all be living under Japanese rule. For days we kept scanning the skies, wondering when they would return. Then, as the days became weeks and our defenses grew stronger, we began to think that maybe they had blundered. Maybe they *wouldn't* return! Maybe we would be safe after all!

In the days preceding that Christmas, there was no time for poring over shopping lists, for checking financial resources, for dashing from one store to another, doing our Christmas shopping. That year we were busy with completely different activities.

Defense stations were immediately set up and throughout the islands. Everyone had to have his blood typed and identification tags were issued. We youngsters thought it was fun to speculate about whose blood we might receive, and we enjoyed comparing blood types. My grandfather claimed his I.D. tag choked him and stubbornly refused to wear it.

We weren't at all excited about the gas masks that became regulation attire. Extremely bulky, they made plump women look even heavier, and awkward children even clumsier. The day that our gas masks were issued to us, my Dad thought it would be a good idea to have a timed drill, so he called everyone to the back yard with their masks. At the word "Go!" we all rushed to get our masks on, and most of us succeeded in just a few seconds.

Poor Grandfather, however, became confused. Instead of whipping his mask out of its case and onto his face, he started to unwind the cording on the case. My brother teased him, "Grandpa, you'd be dead and buried before you got your mask on!" Suddenly it wasn't funny anymore.

We went back into the house, praying that we would never have to use those ugly devices. In later years, the gas-mask cases became handy carryalls—convenient places to deposit hair-brushes, combs, lipsticks and bus tokens—but in those first few weeks, we resented them.

There were no Christmas parties, luaus or other festivities being planned—no rehearsals of Christmas concerts, pageants and carols to keep us busy. Instead we were busy digging bomb shelters. Newspaper articles told us how deep to dig, how to brace the shelters and how to stock them. We couldn't dig down as far as suggested, though, because we lived only two blocks from the ocean and soon struck water. We had to leave a large part of our shelter above the ground. We rounded it off on top so that it looked like a giant mushroom, and my mother stocked the shelter with blankets, first-aid supplies and food.

There were several air-raid warnings, especially in those first days after the attack. As soon as we heard the sirens, we all dashed for the bomb shelter, where we youngsters immediately started eating. It seemed like the right thing to do. After all, that was what the food was for. My mother was always so overjoyed to learn that the airplanes weren't enemy planes that she would cheerfully replenish the food, grateful that we had not needed it for our survival.

It's a mystery to me how Mother and Grandma managed to keep us all well fed. At first there was a desperate shortage of food, and people had to stand in line for hours to get the items that were limited—2 pounds of coffee, 5 pounds of sugar, 10 pounds of potatoes to a family. We hoped that another shipload would arrive soon, but we were never sure if our groceries would have to last for five days or 10 or 15.

Fortunately, there were many in our family to stand in the lines. And while I don't recall an abundance of food, I do remember that Grandma often shared our supplies with our neighbors, while still keeping her own family from ever being hungry.

We were grateful that the fruitcakes had been baked early in November; at least we were assured of *one* Christmas tradition. Fruitcakes and the calendar were all we had to remind us that Christmas was approaching. There were no frosted cookies, no gingerbread men, no popcorn balls, no batches of fudge, no battles over who would lick the pot or be the tester to see if the treat was "fit for human consumption."

We knew that we would have some kind of Christmas; we had already discovered packages hidden under Mother's bed and in her closet. (She believed in shopping early.) But as the weeks went by, we noticed that Mother seemed sadder all the time. We knew that she

Garageman a Hero

was worried about Emory. We wanted to make it a really nice Christmas for her sake. A weekend pass for Emory would have been the nicest gift of all, but since we couldn't arrange that, we wanted everything to be as normal and nice as possible.

No lovely Christmas trees arrived from the mainland as they had in other years. With no sweet-smelling firs or pines to decorate our parlor, we did the next-best thing. We cut six long branches from a palm tree, wired them together, and set them in a bucket of sand so our "tree" would stand upright. For security, we also tied it from the ceiling with some fine thread. Then we placed all our favorite ornaments on the tree—the birds, flowers, stars, ginger-bread people and Santas that we had used and loved every year.

We cut a long strip of butcher paper, and on it we painted an elaborate Christmas mural showing all kinds of yuletide images. A simple manger scene at one end featured Mary, Joseph, the Baby Jesus and Three Kings. It became a bit crowded when we added many shepherds, animals and angels.

The next scene showed people enjoying snow, something we had heard about but had never seen. They were busy skiing, skating, building snowmen, riding in sleighs—doing all the things with snow we had always heard about.

The third scene depicted our own family sitting at a table, eating and drinking. Everyone was there, including Emory.

There was something for everyone on our mural, and it was with great pride that we taped it to the wall behind the tree.

When Mother saw our tree, she stood there for a long moment, studying its frail branches and the mural behind it. Then, in a quavering voice, she murmured, "Back in a minute," and dashed off to her bedroom. When she returned she carried arm-loads of gaily wrapped presents. When these had been arranged under the tree, she brought out her camera and used her last two snaps to take pictures of our tree. "For Emory," she said.

Emory never did see those snapshots. We forgot to mail them. But it didn't matter, because he was there in person on Christmas Eve, clutching a three-day pass. Emory thought our tree was the prettiest one he had ever seen. He couldn't take his eyes off it—and Mother couldn't take her eyes off Emory. Grandma thought he looked a little thin and couldn't wait to start fattening him up.

We stayed awake very late that night— so many people came by to say hello to Emory—and how we enjoyed gathering around him, listening to him tell about the funny things that had happened to him in the Army.

We stayed awake very late that night—so many people came by to say hello to Emory—and how we enjoyed gathering around him, listening to him tell about the funny things that had happened to him in the Army.

We were up early the next morning for Mass. We couldn't wait to thank God for bringing us all together again. I think, too, that we couldn't wait to open our presents. But, "first to church, then to the tree," was the rule of thumb in our house.

Grandma had killed and cleaned one of her prize turkeys a few days before, so we had a very festive dinner that night. Then we gathered at the piano where Mom struggled through our favorite Christmas carols while we tried to keep time to her music.

A few months later, Emory was sent to the mainland to Officers' Training School. From there he was sent to various posts, eventually landing in Europe on D-Day. Axel, my second brother and my Grandfather's namesake, joined the Army as soon as he was old enough. He was sent to Germany just before the war ended there. Grandpa died before the boys returned home.

Bittersweet though it was, the Christmas of 1941 has always been my favorite. I can see it as clearly as if it happened yesterday—that last Christmas we spent together as a complete family. ❋

Santa Came On Horseback

By Bonnie Lee Wells

remember the Idaho winter of 1944 as being one of the coldest, snowiest and bleakest in history! "Try not to take it personally," my dad kept telling me. I was a young wife and mother whose soldier husband was in combat somewhere in Europe. But how could I not take the war personally? After all, I had not received a letter from my husband, Larry, for several weeks.

Consequently, Christmas Eve found me gazing out the window into yet another blizzard, and regretting—and almost resenting—the fact that my parents had picked this year to retire from their business in town and buy an isolated farm. Snowdrifts taller than autos blocked roads. Cattle starved and froze to death in their tracks. Airplanes dropped food to ranchers, and mail piled up as we waited for country roads to be plowed open. And all this in the midst of World War II!

Fortunately, my mother, sister and I had finished our shopping early so Santa wouldn't disappoint my baby boy. All *I* wanted for Christmas was a letter from Larry. But there was no chance of that; Dad couldn't even make it to the mailbox on the tractor. For the first time in my life, I found no joy in the holiday season—and this even though we had cut our own Christmas tree, and the house was warm and festive, permeated by the aroma of pumpkin pie.

Along toward evening, Mother stood at the window, watching for Dad to return to the house from feeding the livestock. "I see something in the distance!" she suddenly exclaimed. "I wonder if it's a deer?"

My sister and I were instantly at her side. "If it's a deer, it's a mighty tall one," my sister said.

"I think it's a man on horseback," I gasped.

Mother hurried to the door, started to open it, then hesitated. "It's probably an Indian from the reservation across the river," she said nervously.

"So what if it is?" my sister said.

"But what could he want?"

"Open the door and we'll find out," I suggested nervously.

From the window, my sister and I watched a tall figure dismount, wrap the reigns around a tree and plod through the snowdrifts toward the house. Only then did Mother crack the door open.

"It's me, Lane Shelman!" a deep voice shouted.

Now Mother flung open the door. "Dear Lord, get in here where it's warm!" she gasped. "You must be half-frozen!"

Lane stomped into the room, looking for all the world like a huge snowman. "Merry Christmas!" he exclaimed.

"Merry Christmas to you, too," Mother responded. "But why on earth are you out on a night like this?"

He smiled straight at me. "Just paying a neighborly visit," he said, his eyes twinkling like Santa's. Then he dug into his deep sheepskin pocket and drawled, "As for you, young Mrs. Wells, I have something here that just might make you smile again."

When I saw the envelope, I let out a little screech. "Is it from Larry?"

"You think if it *wasn't* from him I'd have ventured out in this storm?" he joked.

"Oh, thank you!" I sobbed. Hands trembling, I opened the letter and read it. "He's fine," I murmured. "At least he was when he wrote this letter."

"Now that's what I call borrowing trouble!" Dad teased. In my happiness, I hadn't noticed that he had joined us.

"Think your heart can take another surprise?" Lane asked.

"Is it another letter?" I held my breath, hoping.

"Nope … it's *three* more letters," he said, handing them to me one at a time. "I thought about giving you one every few days, so you'd be easier to live with. But since it's Christmas Eve—happy reading!"

"Oh, thank you, thank you!" I sobbed. "I promise I will never forget you, and how special you made this Christmas Eve!"

"Well," he drawled and laughed, "I should hope not!"

As I read the letters, he and my parents chatted over mugs of hot coffee. "I couldn't get through to the mailbox on the tractor," Dad said. "So how did you manage it?"

"Nothing to it," Lane quipped. "You'll soon learn that a farmer on a tractor can't take the place of an old cowboy on a horse. At least not in a blizzard!"

The room was filled with laughter—and so was my heart. "By next Christmas," I said, suddenly optimistic, "the war will be over and Larry will be home, safe and sound."

Sadly, I was wrong. Not only was the war still raging that next Christmas, but my husband was still in combat. Our little boy was 18 months old when his daddy first held him. As for the promise I had made to a dear friend—when I reflect on the Good Old Days, I still remember the harsh winter when Santa came on horseback. ✵

All I wanted for Christmas was a letter from Larry. But there was no chance of that; Dad couldn't even make it to the mailbox on the tractor.

Unforgettable Christmas

By Iris Thompson

While going through my grand-mother's old trunk of keepsakes, I found a box containing the letters my dad wrote home after entering the Army in 1917. Those letters and several telegrams and newspaper articles that my grandmother saved make me believe that Dec. 25, 1918, surely must have been an unforgettable Christmas for my father and his family.

On Nov. 24, 1918, Dad wrote the following letter to his father from France:

Dear Father,

This being "Dad's Day" when all us fellows are supposed to write, I will try and tell you a little of what has been going on so far, since I came over here.

When we left the states on board the Aquatania, the next to the largest ship afloat, and not knowing what was ahead of us, most were a bit blue and uncertain. This did not last long, however, as we were soon busy getting settled down for the trip and taking in the sights that were new to us, and that was everything to me.

Then came drills for abandoning the ship in case we were torpedoed. When the bugler blows fire call, all the men must get on deck with as little confusion as possible, and get to the boat station, where the boat they were assigned to would be lowered. Each man had a card telling what boat he was assigned to, so that was not hard to do. These drills took place twice a day all the way over.

The weather was fine and the water smooth, so there was no excitement until one morning just as we were getting out of bed. A sub came up just a short distance (30 yards) from the ship, and before they could get set to fire a torpedo, the guns got busy and soon had the periscope shot off. Then the destroyers that were with us took up the chase and dropped a depth bomb, and as we heard later, sank her.

On the eighth day, we sighted land and the next morning were in Liverpool harbor. There we unloaded and took the train to Winchester, where we stayed a few days in a rest camp. From there, I wrote the first letter you received. From there, we went to South Hampton and took the boat for France, landing in Le Havre. Then we went by train to a little village somewhere inland about 50 miles back of the battle line and were drilled for about a month and a half.

On the first of June we were ordered to the front, and went to Chateau Thierry, as you will see by the slip enclosed. Then the excitement commenced. On the fifth of June, we got our first shelling, and from then on it was work all the time.

On the 15th of July the Germans crossed the Marne on us, and it was fight and fight hard to stop them. Success was with us, and in a few days they were on the other side again and going toward Germany. We followed them, and on the 10th of August we were at the Visle River.

One morning about 9 o'clock they sent over an attack of mustard gas. That is where they got me. I was taken to the hospital along with the other wounded.

Since then, I have done nothing but lay around, and enjoy myself as much as possible. After being in the base hospital for two months, I was sent to the Red Cross Hospital here at Margot, a popular summer resort on the seashore near Brest.

The gas burned my body pretty badly and also affected my lungs, as I have been unable to do anything so far, but I am getting along alright now. I'm still taking it easy.

I cannot say too much for the Red Cross, and what they are doing for the boys over here, helping them in every way possible.

I suppose by now you have received word from them letting you know I am getting along well. You see, I have received no mail for five months, and did not know if you were getting my letters or not, but I hoped you were.

When I leave here, I do not know what I will have to do, or where I will get to, or when I will be home again. I hope it will be soon now. Perhaps in time to help do the spring work. I hope so anyway.

Now I hope you are well and OK, so I wish you all a Merry Christmas and Happy New Year.

So bye-bye for now.

With much love to all,
Your son, Paul

Dad had no way of knowing he would arrive in the United States before his letter did, or that the last news his parents had of him came in the form of a telegram of Oct. 1, 1918:

"Deeply regret to inform you that it is officially reported that Private Paul Junge was wounded in action degree undetermined about August eleventh department has no further information."

Later my grandparents received Dad's address book, which an Italian soldier found on the battlefield in France. He picked an address from it at random and mailed it to the United States. It came to relatives living in New York, who forwarded it on.

Only after Dad's homecoming did they learn the full extent of his injuries and the rest of his story: One knee had been badly burned when the mustard gas settled on the water in the mud puddle in which he was kneeling at the time of the attack. He later contracted tuberculosis in his badly burned, weakened lungs, and he wore thick glasses, for he had been blinded for a time.

Since none of the men who survived the attack could see, they had formed a human chain and somehow managed to crawl and stumble into a garbage dump, where they were discovered by some friendly French who took them to the hospital.

It must have been wonderful when, on Christmas Day 1918, my grandparents received a telegram from New York telling them of Dad's arrival there on Dec. 23.

He again wished them a Merry Christmas, and it was one they never forgot. ✳

DRAWN BY
Z. P. NIKOLAKI

Christmas 1944

By Leola Richardson

We celebrated Christmas early in December 1944. Then again, "celebrate" is hardly the proper word; "suffered" describes it better. Bernie, my 18-year-old brother, had five days of leave before being shipped to Germany. Practically *all* able-bodied 18-year-olds were being shipped somewhere. War gloom covered the land.

Schoolchildren collected scrap metal for the war effort. When we had an extra quarter we used it to buy a 25-cent U.S. Savings Stamp. When we had accumulated enough stamps, we traded them in for a $25 U.S. Savings Bond. It cost $18.75.

In music class we sang loudly and proudly: "From the halls of Montezuma to the shores of Tripoli, we fight our country's battles on the land as on the sea."

Sugar was rationed, leather shoes were hard to find, and dress materials were shoddy. Our country's best was poured into supplies for our servicemen. Almost every home displayed stars in a window, one for each member of that household serving in some branch of military service.

Families lived in dread of receiving a yellow envelope delivered by Western Union. All those telegrams began the same way: "We regret to inform you … was seriously (or slightly or fatally) wounded in action. …"

If it said "slightly," that didn't seem so bad. Folks encouraged one another. "Since it says 'slightly,' he must not be very badly hurt. Maybe he'll be sent home."

"Seriously wounded" was somber news. "How serious? Is he badly crippled? Will he die?" Every mail delivery was quickly searched for a letter bringing more details. What joy to finally receive a hand-written note from the wounded one!

Bernie's last five days at home passed quickly. There was so much living to pack into such a short time. The night before his last day home was set for our family's Christmas celebration. We wanted to share it with him.

Our pretend Christmas Eve fell on Dec. 4. Mama cooked all day. She fixed the hen and dressing, and baked a coconut cake to set beside the fruitcake that had been soaking in grape juice for several days. There were candied sweet potatoes, mashed potatoes and giblet gravy, green beans and cranberry salad.

The table was set and we all gathered for the blessing. The plates were served, but the food didn't taste as good as it usually did. A vital ingredient for Christmas dinner was missing: There was no laughter. The big monster of war gloom had squeezed all the merriment from our hearts and left us scared and empty.

The only present I remember from that pretend Christmas Eve was a doll. I had a hard time concealing my disappointment. Her painted eyes stared out from a blank face surrounded by orangy hair. Her straight little arms and legs poked out from a cheaply made, too-long dress. War even made ugly dolls.

But happier times had returned by Christmas 1945. The war was over. Bernie was back home, recovering from his seriously wounded condition. The sun shone brightly and that most important ingredient—laughter—was back at the Christmas dinner table. ✳

A Special Delivery

By Faye Hughes

The Christmas season of 1943 found our family with all five of my brothers and the three sons-in-law all serving our country overseas. My husband had gone overseas the last of November, so I decided to spend Christmas at home with Mom and Dad.

I arrived the morning of Dec. 24 and found a gloomy atmosphere prevailing. Mom said it didn't seem right for us to celebrate since the boys probably couldn't.

I viewed it differently and felt that they would want us to carry on as usual. She finally agreed to let me do a little decorating.

Stored away in a box in the attic, I found a small artificial tree with a strand of lights. Underneath that were a pair of electric candles, the red crepe-paper bell and a drab-looking wreath. Not much to work with, but I set to work.

The bell was unfolded and hung from the dining-room chandelier. The candles were placed in the two front windows and the little tree placed nearby. I put a new red bow and streamers on the wreath and placed it on the door.

With that completed, I baked cookies and made old-fashioned cocoa fudge, loaded with black walnuts from our tree.

As I busied myself around the house, I could hear Mom frequently sighing and saying, "Oh, if Paul could just come home, it would mean so much."

Paul was my oldest brother and had not been home for over three years. After being inducted at Fort Benjamin Harrison, he was immediately sent to Camp Walters, Texas, for basic training. He thought he would get a leave at the end of basic, but instead had been shipped to a base in Alaska.

We received a card with his picture on it on the first of December. The accompanying note expressed his homesickness and desire to come home for Christmas, and he wrote, "… but it will only be in my dreams."

On Christmas Eve the weather was very cold and windy so we stayed in and listened to a few radio programs and retired early. Because the bedroom was unheated, I made a bed on the couch.

The hard-coal burner in the dining room cast a rosy glow through the isinglass windows, lighting up the room. The electric candles reflected on the windowpanes and the tree lights added more cheer. Combined with the aromas from the cookies and fudge, it made a restful atmosphere and soon I fell asleep.

At about 2 a.m., I was awakened by a tall soldier with a duffel bag standing beside the couch. He bent over to get a closer view of my face and said, "Which one are you?" (I had been in an auto accident the year before, which had changed my appearance.)

Upon hearing Paul's voice I reached out to touch his uniform sleeve, thinking I was dreaming. When I realized he was actually there, I stood up and we embraced amidst shouts of joy.

Hearing voices in the living room, Mom got up and, upon seeing Paul, ran to meet him, almost hysterical with joy.

After a while we remembered that Dad was still asleep and went to awaken him.

We sat up the rest of the night, talking, laughing, crying, drinking cocoa and eating cookies and fudge. Christmas for us had really arrived.

The Greyhound driver had left Paul off in front of our house, and noticing the glow of the fireside and lights shining through the windows, he said, "They sure are expecting you."

Paul said, "Ho!—no one knows I'm coming." He had not known himself until he arrived in the state of Washington and was given furlough papers for one month.

It was the best Christmas gift he could have received, and it left us with a warm memory still cherished nearly 60 years later. ❄